THE
BIG
BOOK OF
PASTA

THE BIG BOOK OF PASTA

Your complete guide to cooking
perfect pasta every time

Love Food ® is an imprint of Parragon Books Ltd

Parragon
Queen Street House
4 Queen Street
Bath BA1 1HE, UK

Copyright © Parragon Books Ltd 2008

Love Food ® and the accompanying heart device is a trade mark of Parragon Books Ltd

ISBN 978-1-4075-3015-4

Printed in China

Design by Simon Levy
Photography by Don Last
Food styling by Christine France
Introduction by Linda Doeser

Front cover image © Nation Wong/Corbis

Notes for the reader

This book uses both metric and imperial measurements. Follow the same units of measurement throughout; do not mix metric and imperial. All spoon measurements are level: teaspoons are assumed to be 5 ml, and tablespoons are assumed to be 15 ml. Unless otherwise stated, milk is assumed to be full fat, eggs and individual vegetables are medium, and pepper is freshly ground black pepper.

The times given are an approximate guide only. Preparation times differ according to the techniques used by different people and the cooking times may also vary from those given.

Recipes using raw or very lightly cooked eggs should be avoided by infants, the elderly, pregnant women, convalescents and anyone suffering from an illness. Pregnant and breastfeeding women are advised to avoid eating peanuts and peanut products.

Vegetarians should be aware that some brands of the ready-made ingredients specified in the recipes in the Vegetarian chapter in this book may contain animal products. Always check the packaging before use.

CONTENTS

INTRODUCTION

Pasta is arguably the most useful ingredient to be found in any kitchen. It goes with just about anything else you can think of – from vegetables and cheese to meat and fish. It's equally delicious served with simple, inexpensive sauces or extravagant and luxurious mixtures, and it can be added to soups or form the basis of filling baked dishes. It may be a main meal, a starter or a delightfully different salad.

Pasta is very versatile so it's easy to find fabulous recipes for all occasions and every season of the year. Virtually everyone loves pasta and it's especially popular with children. High in complex carbohydrates, it provides a steady release of energy but contains hardly any fat. Depending on the type of wheat flour used in its manufacture, it can also be a good source of protein, as well as B vitamins, potassium and iron. Moreover, it's economical, convenient and the dried variety keeps well. Huge numbers of pasta dishes can be prepared and cooked within 30 minutes and many take only half that time.

TYPES OF PASTA

There are hundreds of pasta shapes and new ones are being introduced all the time. There are no hard and fast rules about which shape goes with a particular sauce, although there are some traditional partnerships, such as Spaghetti Bolognese and Fettuccine all'Alfredo. However, there are some useful guidelines.

Long, thin pasta, such as spaghetti and linguine, is ideal for seafood sauces and light olive oil or fresh tomato dressings, but cannot really hold thick or chunky sauces. These are better served with pasta shapes that trap the sauce in hollows and ridges – penne (quills), fusilli (spirals) or conchiglie (shells), for example. Flat ribbons, such as tagliatelle, fettuccine and pappardelle, are perfect for rich or creamy sauces.

Baked dishes are often made with lasagne (flat sheets of pasta that can be layered with a variety of sauces) or cannelloni (tubes that can be filled and baked in a sauce). Smaller shapes, such as macaroni and rigatoni, are also often used in baking.

Very small pasta shapes, such as stellete (stars) and anellini (rings), are used in soups, and filled pasta, such as ravioli and tortellini, is also often served in broth.

COOKING PASTA

Most of the recipes in this book are made with dried pasta. If you substitute fresh pasta, the cooking times must be adjusted.

1 Bring a large saucepan of salted water to the boil. Allow 4 litres/7 pints water and 3 tablespoons salt for every 300–400 g/ 10^1/$_2$–14 oz dried pasta.

2 Add the pasta. Don't break up long pasta, such as spaghetti, but gently fold and twist it into the pan – it softens in the water. Bring back to the boil.

3 Start timing the cooking at this point. The water must be boiling, not simmering. Allow 8–10 minutes for unfilled dried pasta and 15–20 minutes

for filled dried pasta. Start checking the pasta several minutes before you think it will be ready by biting a small piece between your front teeth. It should be just firm to the bite – *al dente* – and neither soggy nor hard in the middle.

4 Drain in a colander – it's not necessary to be particularly thorough. Either serve immediately with the sauce or toss with olive oil. If cooked pasta is left to stand, it will become sticky and inedible.

Cook fresh pasta in the same way, but allow only 2–3 minutes from the time the water comes back to the boil for unfilled pasta and 8–10 minutes for filled pasta.

MAKING FRESH PASTA

If you want to make filled pasta, such as tortellini, you will need to prepare the dough yourself. The same basic dough can also be used to make lasagne sheets and a variety of shapes, such as tagliatelle, pappardelle and macaroni. You need no special equipment and the process is both easy and satisfying.

Basic pasta dough

Serves 3–4
Preparation time: 15 minutes, plus
30 minutes to rest

Ingredients

200 g/7 oz strong white flour,
   plus extra for dusting
pinch of salt
2 eggs, lightly beaten
1 tbsp olive oil

1 Sift together the flour and salt onto a work surface and make a well in the centre with your fingers. Pour the eggs and oil into the well then, using the fingers of one hand, gradually incorporate the flour into the liquid.

2 Knead the dough on a lightly floured work surface until it is completely smooth. Wrap in clingfilm and leave to rest for 30 minutes before rolling out or feeding through a pasta machine. Resting makes the dough more elastic.

Flavoured pasta

Basic pasta dough may be flavoured and coloured by the addition of other ingredients.

Tomato pasta: Add 2 tablespoons of tomato purée to the well in the flour and use only $1^1/_2$ eggs instead of 2.

Spinach pasta: Blanch 225 g/8 oz spinach in boiling water for 1 minute, then drain and squeeze out as much liquid as possible. Alternatively, use 150 g/$5^1/_2$ oz thawed frozen spinach. This does not need blanching, but as much liquid as possible should be squeezed out. Finely chop the spinach and mix with the flour before making a well and adding the eggs and oil.

Herb pasta: Add 3 tablespoons of finely chopped fresh herbs to the flour before making a well and adding the eggs and oil.

Saffron pasta: Soak a sachet of powdered saffron in 2 tablespoons hot water for 15 minutes. Use $1^1/_2$ eggs and whisk the saffron water into them.

Wholemeal pasta: Use 140 g/5 oz wholemeal flour and 25 g/1 oz strong white flour.

Rolling out pasta dough

When the fresh dough has rested, it may be rolled out by hand or with a pasta machine. Larger quantities of dough should be halved or cut into thirds before rolling out. Keep covered until you are ready to work on them.

To roll out by hand, lightly dust a work surface with plain flour, then roll out the pasta dough with a lightly floured rolling pin, always rolling away from you and turning the dough a quarter turn each time. Keep rolling to make a rectangle 2–3 mm/ $^1/_{16}$–$^1/_8$ inch thick. The dough can then be cut into ribbons, stamped out with a biscuit cutter or cut into squares to make ravioli.

A pasta machine makes rolling out the dough easier and quicker and ensures that it is even. There are a number of models available, the most useful being a hand-cranked machine with attachable cutters. An electric machine is even easier to use but somewhat extravagant. Cut the dough into manageable sized pieces – 1 quantity Basic Pasta Dough should be cut into 4 pieces, for example. Flatten a piece with your hand and wrap the others in clingfilm until required. Fold the flat piece into thirds and feed it through the pasta machine on its widest setting. Repeat the folding and rolling 3 or 4 more times on this setting, then close the rollers by one notch. Continue feeding the dough through the rollers, without folding into thirds, gradually reducing the setting until you reach the narrowest. If you want to make ribbons, cut the dough into 30-cm/12-inch strips and feed through the appropriate cutter.

Cutting and shaping fresh pasta

Pasta machines usually have a wide cutter for tagliatelle and a narrower one for tagliarini. Other pasta shapes can be cut by hand.

To make pappardelle, use a serrated pasta wheel to cut 2.5 cm/1 inch wide ribbons from the rolled-out dough. To make tagliatelle or tagliarini, roll up a strip of dough like a Swiss roll and then cut into 5-mm/^{1}/$_4$-inch slices (tagliatelle) or 3-mm/^{1}/$_8$-inch slices (tagliarini) with a sharp knife. To make macaroni, cut the pasta dough into 2.5-cm/1-inch squares with a sharp knife, then roll them corner to corner around a chopstick to form tubes. Slide off and leave to dry slightly.

Italians use the word *ravioli* as an all-purpose term for filled pasta and it can, therefore, be a variety of shapes.

Half-moon ravioli

1 Roll out the pasta dough to 2–3 mm/ ^{1}/$_{16}$–^{1}/$_8$ inch thick. Using a 5-cm/2-inch fluted biscuit cutter, stamp out rounds.

2 Place about 1 teaspoon of prepared filling in the centre, brush the edges of each round with a little water or beaten egg, then fold in half, pressing the edges to seal.

3 Place on a floured tea towel and leave to stand for 30–60 minutes to dry out slightly before cooking.

Ravioli rounds

1 Roll out the pasta dough to 2–3 mm/ ^{1}/$_{16}$–^{1}/$_8$ inch thick. Using a 5-cm/2-inch plain biscuit cutter, stamp out rounds.

2 Place about 1^1/$_2$–2 teaspoons of the filling on half the rounds. Brush the edges with a little water or beaten egg, then cover with the remaining rounds, pressing the edges to seal.

3 Place on a floured tea towel and leave to stand for 30–60 minutes to dry out slightly before cooking.

Square ravioli

1 Divide the pasta dough in half and wrap 1 piece in clingfilm. Roll out the other piece to a rectangle 2–3 mm/^{1}/16–^{1}/8 inch thick. Cover with a damp tea towel and roll out the other piece of dough to the same size.

2 Place 1 teaspoon of the filling in neat rows spaced about 4 cm/1^1/2 inches apart on a sheet of pasta dough. Brush the spaces between the mounds with a little water or beaten egg.

3 Using a rolling pin, place the second sheet of dough on top and press down firmly between the pockets of filling, pushing out any air bubbles. Using a pasta wheel or sharp knife, cut into squares.

4 Place on a floured tea towel and leave to stand for 30–60 minutes to dry out slightly before cooking.

Tortellini

There are several legends about the origins of these little pasta twists. One is that a cook, seeing his employer's naked wife asleep, fell hopelessly in love with her. As a tribute, he made filled pasta in the shape of her navel. In another version of the story, tortellini are said to have been inspired by the navel of Venus, goddess of love.

1 Roll out the pasta dough to 2–3 mm/ ^{1}/16–^{1}/8 inch thick. Using a 5-cm/2-inch plain biscuit cutter, stamp out rounds.

2 Place about 1 teaspoon of the filling in the centre of each round. Brush the edges of each round with a little water or beaten egg, then fold them in half to make half moons and press the edges to seal.

3 Wrap a half moon around the tip of your index finger until the corners meet and press them together to seal. Repeat with the remaining pasta half moons. Place the filled tortellini on a floured tea towel and leave to stand for 30–60 minutes to dry out slightly before cooking.

BASIC RECIPES

Tomato Sauce

Serves 4

Ingredients
2 tbsp olive oil
1 small onion, chopped
1 garlic clove, finely chopped
400 g/14 oz canned chopped tomatoes
2 tbsp chopped fresh flat-leaf parsley
1 tsp dried oregano
2 bay leaves
2 tbsp tomato purée
1 tsp sugar
salt and pepper

1 Heat the oil in a saucepan. Add the onion and garlic and cook over a low heat, stirring occasionally, for 5 minutes, until softened.

2 Increase the heat to medium, stir in the tomatoes, parsley, oregano, bay leaves, tomato purée and sugar, and season to taste with salt and pepper.

3 Bring to the boil, then lower the heat and simmer, uncovered, for 15–20 minutes, until reduced by half. Taste and adjust the seasoning, if necessary, and remove and discard the bay leaves.

Ragù alla Bolognese (Bolognese Meat Sauce)

Serves 4–6

Ingredients
3 tbsp olive oil
40 g/1^1/$_2$ oz butter
175 g/6 oz pancetta or bacon, diced
2 large onions, chopped
2 celery sticks, chopped
2 carrots, chopped
2 garlic cloves, finely chopped
500 g/1 lb 2 oz lean beef mince
2 tbsp tomato purée
400 g/14 oz canned chopped tomatoes
150 ml/5 fl oz Beef Stock (see page 14)
150 ml/5 fl oz red wine
2 tsp dried oregano
salt and pepper

1 Heat the oil and butter in a heavy-based saucepan. Add the pancetta and cook over a low heat, stirring frequently, for 2–3 minutes. Add the onions, celery and carrots and cook, stirring occasionally, for a further 5 minutes, until softened.

2 Increase the heat to medium, add the garlic and beef and cook, stirring frequently, until the meat is evenly browned. Lower the heat and cook, stirring frequently, for a further 10 minutes.

3 Increase the heat to medium, stir in the tomato purée, tomatoes, stock and wine and bring to the boil, stirring constantly. Season to taste with salt and pepper, stir in the oregano and lower the heat. Cover and simmer very gently, stirring occasionally, for 45 minutes. Taste and adjust the seasoning before using.

Béchamel Sauce

Makes 300 ml/10 fl oz

Ingredients
300 ml/10 fl oz milk
1 bay leaf
6 black peppercorns
slice of onion
mace blade
25 g/1 oz butter
25 g/1 oz plain flour
salt and pepper

1 Pour the milk into a saucepan and add the bay leaf, peppercorns, onion and mace. Bring to just below boiling point, then remove the pan from the heat, cover and leave to infuse for 10 minutes. Strain the milk into a jug and discard the flavourings.

2 Melt the butter in another saucepan. Sprinkle in the flour and cook over a low heat, stirring constantly, for 2 minutes. Remove the pan from the heat and gradually stir in the milk.

3 Return the pan to a low heat and bring to the boil, stirring constantly. Cook, stirring constantly, until thickened and smooth. Season to taste with salt and pepper.

Pesto

Serves 4

Ingredients
115 g/4 oz fresh basil leaves
25 g/1 oz pine kernels
1 garlic clove, roughly chopped
55 g/2 oz Parmesan cheese, freshly grated
6–8 tbsp extra virgin olive oil
salt

1 Put the basil, pine kernels and garlic in a mortar. Add a pinch of salt and pound to a paste with a pestle.

2 Transfer the mixture to a bowl and gradually work in the Parmesan cheese with a wooden spoon. Gradually stir in the oil until the sauce is thick and creamy. Cover with clingfilm and store in the refrigerator until required.

Beef Stock

Makes 1.7 litres/3 pints

Ingredients

1 kg/2 lb 4 oz beef marrow bones, sawn into
   7.5-cm/3-inch pieces
650 g/1 lb 7 oz stewing beef in a single piece
2.8 litres/5 pints water
4 cloves
2 onions, halved
2 celery sticks, roughly chopped
8 peppercorns
1 bouquet garni

1 Put the bones in a large heavy-based
   saucepan and put the stewing beef on top.
   Pour in the water and bring to the boil over
   a low heat. Skim off the scum that rises to
   the surface.

2 Press a clove into each onion half and add
   to the pan with the celery, peppercorns and
   bouquet garni. Partially cover and simmer
   gently for 3 hours. Remove the stewing beef
   from the pan, partially re-cover and simmer
   for a further hour.

3 Remove the pan from the heat and leave to
   cool. Strain the stock into a bowl, cover with
   clingfilm and chill in the refrigerator for at
   least 1 hour and preferably overnight.

4 Remove and discard the layer of fat that has
   set on the surface. Use immediately or freeze
   for up to 6 months.

Chicken Stock

Makes 2.5 litres/4^{1}/$_{2}$ pints

Ingredients

1.3 kg/3 lb chicken wings and necks
2 onions, cut into wedges
4 litres/7 pints water
2 carrots, roughly chopped
2 celery sticks, roughly chopped
10 fresh parsley sprigs
4 fresh thyme sprigs
2 bay leaves
10 black peppercorns

1 Place the chicken and onions in a large
   heavy-based saucepan and cook over a low
   heat, stirring frequently, until browned all over.

2 Pour in the water and stir well, scraping up
   any sediment from the base of the pan. Bring
   to the boil and skim off the scum that rises to
   the surface.

3 Add the carrots, celery, parsley, thyme, bay
   leaves and peppercorns, partially cover the
   pan and simmer gently, stirring occasionally,
   for 3 hours.

4 Remove the pan from the heat and leave to
   cool. Strain the stock into a bowl, cover with
   clingfilm and chill in the refrigerator for at
   least 1 hour and preferably overnight.

5 Remove and discard the layer of fat that has
   set on the surface. Use immediately or freeze
   for up to 6 months.

Fish Stock

Makes 1.3 litres/2¹/₄ pints

Ingredients
650 g/1 lb 7 oz white fish heads, bones
   and trimmings
1 onion, sliced
2 celery sticks, chopped
1 carrot, sliced
1 bay leaf
4 fresh parsley sprigs
4 black peppercorns
¹/₂ lemon, sliced
125 ml/4 fl oz dry white wine
1.3 litres/2¹/₄ pints water

1 Cut out and discard the gills from the fish
heads, then rinse the heads, bones and
trimmings. Place them in a large heavy-
based saucepan.

2 Add all the remaining ingredients. Bring to the
boil and skim off the scum that rises to the
surface. Lower the heat, partially cover and
simmer gently for 25 minutes.

3 Remove the pan from the heat and leave to
cool. Strain the stock into a bowl, without
pressing down on the contents of the colander.
Use immediately or freeze for up to 3 months.

Vegetable Stock

Makes 2 litres/3¹/₂ pints

Ingredients
2 tbsp sunflower or corn oil
115 g/4 oz onions, finely chopped
115 g/4 oz leeks, finely chopped
115 g/4 oz carrots, finely chopped
4 celery sticks, finely chopped
85 g/3 oz fennel, finely chopped
85 g/3 oz tomatoes, finely chopped
2.25 litres/4 pints water
1 bouquet garni

1 Heat the oil in a large heavy-based saucepan.
Add the onions and leeks and cook over a low
heat, stirring occasionally, for 5 minutes, until
softened.

2 Add the carrots, celery, fennel and tomatoes,
cover and cook, stirring occasionally, for
10 minutes. Pour in the water, add the
bouquet garni and bring to the boil. Lower
the heat and simmer for 20 minutes.

3 Remove the pan from the heat and leave to
cool. Strain the stock into a bowl. Use
immediately or freeze for up to 3 months.

SOUPS & SALADS

MINESTRONE MILANESE

Heat the oil in a large heavy-based saucepan. Add the pancetta, onions and garlic and cook, stirring occasionally, for 5 minutes. Add the carrots and celery and cook, stirring occasionally, for a further 5 minutes, or until all the vegetables are softened.

Drain the haricot beans and add them to the saucepan with the tomatoes and their can juices and the beef stock. Bring to the boil, reduce the heat, cover and simmer for 1 hour.

Add the potatoes, re-cover and cook for 15 minutes, then add the pasta, green beans, peas, cabbage and parsley. Cover and cook for a further 15 minutes, until all the vegetables are tender. Season to taste with salt and pepper. Ladle into warmed soup bowls and serve immediately with Parmesan cheese shavings.

SERVES 6

2 tbsp olive oil

55 g/2 oz pancetta, diced

2 onions, sliced

2 garlic cloves, finely chopped

3 carrots, chopped

2 celery sticks, chopped

225 g/8 oz haricot beans,
    soaked for 3–4 hours

400 g/14 oz canned chopped
    tomatoes

2 litres/3½ pints beef stock

350 g/12 oz potatoes, diced

175 g/6 oz dried macaroni

175 g/6 oz green beans, sliced

115 g/4 oz fresh or frozen peas

225 g/8 oz Savoy cabbage,
    shredded

3 tbsp chopped fresh flat-leaf
    parsley

salt and pepper

fresh Parmesan cheese shavings,
    to serve

TOMATO BROTH WITH ANGEL HAIR PASTA

Put the tomatoes, garlic cloves, onion, saffron, sugar, bouquet garni and lemon rind into a large heavy-based saucepan. Pour in the stock and bring to the boil, then lower the heat, cover and simmer, stirring occasionally, for 25–30 minutes, until the tomatoes have disintegrated.

Remove the pan from the heat and leave to cool slightly. Remove and discard the garlic cloves, bouquet garni and lemon rind. Ladle the tomato mixture into a food processor or blender and process to a purée.

Return the purée to the rinsed-out pan and season to taste with salt and pepper. Stir in the oil and bring to the boil. Add the pasta, bring back to the boil and cook for 2–4 minutes, until tender but still firm to the bite.

Taste and adjust the seasoning, if necessary. Ladle the broth and pasta into warmed soup bowls and serve immediately.

SERVES 4

500 g/1 lb 2 oz ripe tomatoes, peeled and halved

8 garlic cloves, peeled but left whole

1 Spanish onion, chopped

½ tsp saffron threads, lightly crushed

1 tsp sugar

1 bouquet garni

5-cm/2-inch strip thinly pared lemon rind

600 ml/1 pint vegetable or chicken stock

2 tbsp extra virgin olive oil

280 g/10 oz dried angel hair pasta

salt and pepper

BROWN LENTIL
& PASTA SOUP

SERVES 4

4 rashers streaky bacon, cut into
small squares

1 onion, chopped

2 garlic cloves, crushed

2 celery sticks, chopped

50 g/1¾ oz dried farfalline

400 g/14 oz canned brown lentils,
drained

1.2 litres/2 pints vegetable stock

2 tbsp chopped fresh mint,
plus extra sprigs to garnish

Place the bacon in a large frying pan together with the onion,
garlic and celery. Dry-fry for 4–5 minutes, stirring, until the onion
is tender and the bacon is just beginning to brown.

Add the pasta to the frying pan and cook, stirring, for 1 minute
to coat the pasta in the fat.

Add the lentils and the vegetable stock and bring to the boil.
Reduce the heat and leave to simmer for 12–15 minutes, or until
the pasta is tender but still firm to the bite.

Remove the frying pan from the heat and stir in the chopped
fresh mint. Transfer the soup to warmed soup bowls, garnish with
fresh mint sprigs and serve immediately.

TUSCAN BEAN
SOUP

Place half the cannellini beans and half the borlotti beans in a food processor with half the stock and process until smooth. Pour into a large heavy-based saucepan and add the remaining beans. Stir in enough of the remaining stock to achieve the consistency you like, then bring to the boil.

Add the pasta and return to the boil, then reduce the heat and cook for 15 minutes, or until just tender.

Meanwhile, heat 3 tablespoons of the oil in a small frying pan. Add the garlic and cook, stirring constantly, for 2–3 minutes, or until golden. Stir the garlic into the soup with the parsley.

Season to taste with salt and pepper and ladle into warmed soup bowls. Drizzle with the remaining oil to taste and serve immediately.

SERVES 6

300 g/10½ oz canned cannellini beans, drained and rinsed

300 g/10½ oz canned borlotti beans, drained and rinsed

about 600 ml/1 pint chicken or vegetable stock

115 g/4 oz dried conchigliette

4–5 tbsp olive oil

2 garlic cloves, very finely chopped

3 tbsp chopped fresh flat-leaf parsley

salt and pepper

BEAN & PASTA SOUP

Put the beans into a large pan, cover with cold water and bring to the boil. Boil rapidly for 10 minutes to remove any toxins. Drain and rinse.

Heat the oil in a large pan over a medium heat. Add the onions and cook until they are just starting to change colour. Stir in the garlic and cook for a further minute. Stir in the chopped tomatoes, oregano and the tomato purée. Pour over the water.

Add the cooked, drained beans to the mixture in the pan, bring to the boil and cover. Simmer for about 45 minutes, or until the beans are almost tender.

Add the pasta, season to taste with salt and pepper and stir in the sun-dried tomatoes. Return the soup to the boil, partially cover and continue cooking for 10 minutes, or until the pasta is nearly tender.

Stir in the chopped coriander. Taste the soup and adjust the seasoning, if necessary. Ladle the soup into warmed soup bowls, sprinkle with the Parmesan cheese and serve immediately.

SERVES 4

225 g/8 oz dried haricot beans, soaked, drained and rinsed

4 tbsp olive oil

2 large onions, sliced

3 garlic cloves, chopped

400 g/14 oz canned chopped tomatoes

1 tsp dried oregano

1 tsp tomato purée

850 ml/1½ pints water

85 g/3 oz dried macaroni

125 g/4½ oz sun-dried tomatoes, drained and thinly sliced

1 tbsp chopped fresh coriander or flat-leaf parsley

2 tbsp freshly grated Parmesan cheese

salt and pepper

POTATO & PESTO SOUP

SERVES 4

2 tbsp olive oil

3 rashers rindless, smoked bacon, finely chopped

25 g/1 oz butter

450 g/1 lb floury potatoes, chopped

450 g/1 lb onions, finely chopped

600 ml/1 pint chicken stock

600 ml/1 pint milk

100 g/3½ oz dried conchigliette

150 ml/5 fl oz double cream

2 tbsp chopped parsley

2 tbsp Pesto (see page 13)

salt and pepper

freshly grated Parmesan cheese, to serve

Heat the oil in a large saucepan and cook the bacon over a medium heat for 4 minutes. Add the butter, potatoes and onions and cook for 12 minutes, stirring constantly.

Add the stock and milk to the saucepan, bring to the boil and simmer for 5 minutes. Add the conchigliette and simmer for a further 3–4 minutes.

Blend in the cream and simmer for 5 minutes. Add the parsley, salt and pepper to taste and pesto. Transfer the soup to individual serving bowls and serve with Parmesan cheese.

FRESH TOMATO SOUP

Heat the oil in a large heavy-based saucepan and add the tomatoes, onion, garlic and celery. Cover and cook over a low heat for 45 minutes, occasionally shaking the saucepan gently, until the mixture is pulpy.

Transfer the mixture to a food processor or blender and process to a smooth purée. Push the purée through a sieve into the rinsed-out saucepan.

Add the stock and bring to the boil. Add the pasta, bring back to the boil and cook for 8–10 minutes, until the pasta is tender but still firm to the bite. Season to taste with salt and pepper. Ladle into warmed bowls, sprinkle with the parsley and serve immediately.

SERVES 4

1 tbsp olive oil

650 g/1 lb 7 oz plum tomatoes

1 onion, cut into quarters

1 garlic clove, thinly sliced

1 celery stick, roughly chopped

500 ml/18 fl oz chicken stock

55 g/2 oz dried macaroni

salt and pepper

chopped fresh flat-leaf parsley,
  to garnish

ITALIAN
CHICKEN SOUP

Place the chicken in a large saucepan and pour in the chicken stock and cream. Bring to the boil, then reduce the heat and simmer for 20 minutes.

Meanwhile, bring a large heavy-based saucepan of lightly salted water to the boil. Add the pasta, return to the boil and cook for 8–10 minutes, or until just tender but still firm to the bite. Drain the pasta well and keep warm.

Season the soup with salt and pepper to taste. Mix the cornflour and milk together until a smooth paste forms, then stir it into the soup. Add the sweetcorn and pasta and heat through. Ladle the soup into warmed soup bowls and serve.

SERVES 4

450 g/1 lb skinless, boneless chicken breasts, cut into thin strips

1.2 litres/2 pints chicken stock

150 ml/5 fl oz double cream

115 g/4 oz dried vermicelli

1 tbsp cornflour

3 tbsp milk

175 g/6 oz canned sweetcorn kernels, drained

salt and pepper

CHICKEN & PASTA BROTH

SERVES 4–6

1.25 kg/2 lb 12 oz chicken pieces, such as wings or legs

2.5 litres/4½ pints water

1 celery stick, sliced

1 large carrot, sliced

1 onion, sliced

1 leek, sliced

2 garlic cloves, finely chopped

8 peppercorns

4 allspice berries

3–4 fresh parsley stems

2–3 fresh thyme sprigs

1 bay leaf

85 g/3 oz dried farfalline

salt and pepper

chopped fresh parsley, to garnish

Put the chicken into a large flameproof casserole dish with the water, celery, carrot, onion, leek, garlic, peppercorns, allspice, herbs and ½ teaspoon of salt. Bring just to the boil over a medium heat and skim off the scum that rises to the surface. Reduce the heat, partially cover and simmer for 2 hours.

Remove the chicken from the stock and leave to cool. Continue simmering the stock, uncovered, for about 30 minutes. When the chicken is cool enough to handle, remove the meat from the bones and, if necessary, cut into bite-sized pieces.

Strain the stock and remove as much fat as possible. Discard the vegetables and flavourings. (There should be about 1.7 litres/ 3 pints chicken stock.)

Bring the stock to the boil in a clean pan over a medium heat. Add the pasta and reduce the heat so the stock simmers very gently. Cook for 8–10 minutes, or until the pasta is tender but still firm to the bite.

Stir in the chicken. Taste and adjust the seasoning. Ladle into bowls, sprinkle with parsley and serve.

CHICKEN & BEAN SOUP

Melt the butter in a large pan over a medium heat. Add the spring onions, garlic, marjoram and chicken and cook, stirring frequently, for 5 minutes.

Add the chicken stock, chickpeas and bouquet garni. Season to taste with salt and white pepper.

Bring the soup to the boil over a medium heat. Reduce the heat and simmer for about 2 hours.

Add the diced peppers and pasta to the pan, then simmer for a further 20 minutes.

Ladle the soup into warmed serving bowls and sprinkle over the croûtons. Serve immediately.

SERVES 4

2 tbsp butter

3 spring onions, chopped

2 garlic cloves, crushed

1 fresh marjoram sprig, finely chopped

350 g/12 oz chicken breasts, diced

1.2 litres/2 pints chicken stock

350 g/12 oz canned chickpeas, drained and rinsed

1 bouquet garni

1 red pepper, diced

1 green pepper, diced

115 g/4 oz dried macaroni

salt and white pepper

croûtons, to serve

TUSCAN VEAL BROTH

Put the peas, veal, stock and water into a large pan and bring to the boil over a low heat. Using a slotted spoon, skim off any scum that rises to the surface.

When all of the scum has been removed, add the pearl barley and a pinch of salt to the mixture. Simmer gently over a low heat for 25 minutes.

Add the carrot, turnip, leek, onion, tomatoes and basil to the pan, and season to taste with salt and white pepper. Simmer for about 2 hours, skimming the surface from time to time to remove any scum. Remove the pan from the heat and set aside for 2 hours.

Set the pan over a medium heat and bring to the boil. Add the vermicelli and cook for 8–10 minutes. Season to taste with salt and white pepper, then remove and discard the basil. Ladle into soup bowls and serve immediately.

SERVES 4

55 g/2 oz dried peas, soaked for 2 hours and drained

900 g/2 lb boned neck of veal, diced

1.2 litres/2 pints beef stock

600 ml/1 pint water

55 g/2 oz pearl barley, washed

1 large carrot, diced

1 small turnip (about 175 g/6 oz), diced

1 large leek, thinly sliced

1 red onion, finely chopped

100 g/3½ oz chopped tomatoes

1 fresh basil sprig

100 g/3½ oz dried vermicelli

salt and white pepper

TORTELLINI IN BROTH

SERVES 6

3 tbsp olive oil

1 red onion, finely chopped

2 garlic cloves, finely chopped

350 g/12 oz fresh beef mince

1 tsp finely chopped fresh thyme

1 fresh rosemary sprig, finely
  chopped

1 bay leaf

1.7 litres/3 pints beef stock

2 quantities Basic Pasta Dough
  (see page 8)

plain flour, for dusting

1 egg, lightly beaten

salt and pepper

Heat the oil in a saucepan. Add the onion and garlic and cook over a low heat, stirring occasionally, for 5 minutes, until softened but not browned. Add the beef, increase the heat to medium and cook, stirring with a wooden spoon to break up the meat, for 8–10 minutes, until evenly browned.

Stir in the herbs, season to taste with salt and pepper, add 125 ml/4 fl oz of the stock and bring to the boil. Cover and simmer for 25 minutes, then remove the lid and cook until all the liquid has evaporated. Remove from the heat and discard the bay leaf.

Roll out the pasta dough on a lightly floured surface to 2–3 mm/$\frac{1}{16}$–$\frac{1}{8}$ inch thick. Using a 2-cm/$\frac{3}{4}$-inch plain biscuit cutter, stamp out rounds. Place about $\frac{1}{4}$ teaspoon of the meat mixture in the centre of each round.

Brush the edges of each round with a little beaten egg, then fold them in half to make half moons and press the edges to seal. Wrap a half moon around the tip of your index finger until the corners meet and press together to seal. Repeat with the remaining pasta half moons. Place the filled tortellini on a floured tea towel and leave to dry for 30 minutes.

Bring the remaining stock to the boil in a large saucepan. Add the tortellini, bring back to the boil and cook for 3–4 minutes, until tender but still firm to the bite. Ladle the tortellini and broth into warmed soup bowls and serve immediately.

FISH SOUP WITH MACARONI

Heat the oil in a large heavy-based saucepan. Add the onions and garlic and cook over a low heat, stirring occasionally, for 5 minutes, or until the onions have softened.

Add the stock with the tomatoes and their can juices, herbs, saffron and pasta and season to taste with salt and pepper. Bring to the boil, then cover and simmer for 15 minutes.

Discard any mussels with broken shells or any that refuse to close when tapped. Add the mussels, monkfish and prawns to the saucepan. Re-cover the saucepan and simmer for a further 5–10 minutes, until the mussels have opened, the prawns have changed colour and the fish is opaque and flakes easily. Discard any mussels that remain closed. Ladle the soup into warmed bowls and serve.

SERVES 6

2 tbsp olive oil

2 onions, sliced

1 garlic clove, finely chopped

1 litre/1¾ pints fish stock or water

400 g/14 oz canned chopped tomatoes

¼ tsp herbes de Provence

¼ tsp saffron threads

115 g/4 oz dried macaroni

18 live mussels, scrubbed and debearded

450 g/1 lb monkfish fillet, cut into chunks

225 g/8 oz raw prawns, peeled and deveined, tails left on

salt and pepper

MUSSEL & PASTA SOUP

Discard any mussels with broken shells or any that refuse to close when tapped. Bring a large heavy-based saucepan of water to the boil. Add the mussels and oil and season to taste with pepper. Cover tightly and cook over a high heat for 5 minutes, or until the mussels have opened. Remove the mussels with a slotted spoon, discarding any that remain closed. Strain the cooking liquid through a muslin-lined sieve and reserve 1.2 litres/2 pints.

Melt the butter in a clean saucepan. Add the bacon, onion and garlic and cook over a low heat, stirring occasionally, for 5 minutes. Stir in the flour and cook, stirring, for 1 minute. Gradually stir in all but 2 tablespoons of the reserved cooking liquid and bring to the boil, stirring constantly. Add the potato slices and simmer for 5 minutes. Add the pasta and simmer for a further 10 minutes.

Stir in the cream and lemon juice and season to taste with salt and pepper. Add the mussels. Mix the egg yolks and the remaining mussel cooking liquid together, then stir the mixture into the soup and cook for 4 minutes, until thickened.

Ladle the soup into warmed soup bowls, garnish with chopped parsley and serve immediately.

SERVES 4

750 g/1 lb 10 oz mussels, scrubbed and debearded

2 tbsp olive oil

100 g/3½ oz butter

55 g/2 oz rindless streaky bacon, chopped

1 onion, chopped

2 garlic cloves, finely chopped

55 g/2 oz plain flour

3 potatoes, thinly sliced

115 g/4 oz dried farfalle

300 ml/10 fl oz double cream

1 tbsp lemon juice

2 egg yolks

salt and pepper

2 tbsp finely chopped fresh parsley, to garnish

AVOCADO, TOMATO & MOZZARELLA SALAD

SERVES 4

2 tbsp pine kernels

175 g/6 oz dried fusilli

6 tomatoes

225 g/8 oz mozzarella cheese

1 large avocado

2 tbsp lemon juice

3 tbsp chopped fresh basil, plus
   extra sprigs to garnish

salt and pepper

dressing

6 tbsp extra virgin olive oil

2 tbsp white wine vinegar

1 tsp wholegrain mustard

pinch of sugar

salt and pepper

Spread the pine kernels out on a baking tray and toast under a preheated hot grill for 1–2 minutes. Remove and leave to cool.

Bring a large pan of lightly salted water to the boil over a medium heat. Add the pasta and cook for 8–10 minutes, or until tender but still firm to the bite. Drain the pasta and refresh in cold water. Drain again and leave to cool.

Thinly slice the tomatoes and the mozzarella cheese.

Using a sharp knife, cut the avocado in half, remove the stone and skin, then cut into thin slices lengthways. Sprinkle with lemon juice to prevent discoloration.

To make the dressing, whisk the oil, vinegar, mustard and sugar together in a small bowl. Season to taste with salt and pepper.

Arrange the sliced tomatoes, mozzarella cheese and avocado alternately in overlapping slices on a large serving platter.

Toss the pasta with half the dressing and the chopped basil and season to taste with salt and pepper. Spoon the pasta onto the platter and pour over the remaining dressing. Sprinkle over the pine kernels and garnish with fresh basil sprigs. Serve immediately.

GOAT'S CHEESE, PEAR & WALNUT SALAD

Bring a large pan of lightly salted water to the boil over a medium heat. Add the pasta and cook for about 8–10 minutes, or until tender but still firm to the bite. Drain the pasta, refresh under cold running water, drain again and leave to cool.

Put the radicchio and Webbs lettuce into a large salad bowl and mix together well. Top with the cooled pasta, walnuts, pears and rocket.

Mix the lemon juice, oil, garlic and vinegar together in a measuring jug. Pour the mixture over the salad ingredients and toss to coat the salad leaves thoroughly.

Add the tomato wedges, onion slices, grated carrot and diced goat's cheese and, using 2 forks, toss together until well mixed. Leave the salad to chill in the refrigerator for about 1 hour before serving.

SERVES 4

250 g/9 oz dried penne

1 head radicchio, torn into pieces

1 Webbs lettuce, torn into pieces

7 tbsp chopped walnuts

2 ripe pears, cored and diced

115 g/4 oz rocket

2 tbsp lemon juice

5 tbsp olive oil

1 garlic clove, chopped

3 tbsp white wine vinegar

4 tomatoes, cut into wedges

1 small onion, sliced

1 large carrot, grated

250 g/9 oz goat's cheese, diced

salt

PASTA SALAD WITH WALNUTS & DOLCELATTE

Bring a large heavy-based saucepan of lightly salted water to the boil. Add the pasta, return to the boil and cook for 8–10 minutes, or until tender but still firm to the bite. Drain and refresh in a bowl of cold water. Drain again.

Mix the walnut oil, safflower oil and vinegar together in a jug, whisking well, and season to taste with salt and pepper.

Arrange the salad leaves in a large serving bowl. Top with the pasta, dolcelatte cheese and walnuts. Pour the dressing over the salad, toss lightly and serve.

SERVES 4

225 g/8 oz dried farfalle

2 tbsp walnut oil

4 tbsp safflower oil

2 tbsp balsamic vinegar

280 g/10 oz mixed salad leaves

225 g/8 oz dolcelatte cheese, diced

115 g/4 oz walnut halves, toasted

salt and pepper

PENNE & APPLE SALAD

SERVES 4

2 large lettuces

250 g/9 oz dried penne

8 red apples, diced

juice of 4 lemons

1 head of celery, sliced

115 g/4 oz walnut halves

250 ml/9 fl oz fresh garlic
    mayonnaise

salt and pepper

Wash and drain the lettuce leaves, then pat them dry with kitchen paper. Transfer them to the refrigerator for 1 hour, or until crisp.

Meanwhile, bring a large saucepan of lightly salted water to the boil. Add the pasta, bring back to the boil and cook for 8–10 minutes, or until tender but still firm to the bite. Drain the pasta and refresh under cold running water. Drain thoroughly and cool.

Core and dice the apples, place them in a bowl and sprinkle with the lemon juice to coat them thoroughly – this will prevent discoloration. Mix together the cooled pasta, celery, apples and walnut halves and toss the mixture in the garlic mayonnaise. Season to taste with salt and pepper.

Line a salad bowl with the lettuce leaves and spoon the pasta salad on top. Refrigerate until ready to serve.

PASTA SALAD
WITH PESTO
VINAIGRETTE

Bring a large pan of lightly salted water to the boil over a medium heat. Add the pasta and cook for about 8–10 minutes, or until tender but still firm to the bite. Drain, rinse in hot water, then drain again and reserve.

To make the pesto vinaigrette, whisk the basil, garlic, Parmesan cheese, oil and lemon juice together in a small bowl until well blended. Season to taste with pepper.

Put the pasta into a bowl, pour over the pesto vinaigrette and toss thoroughly.

Cut the tomatoes into wedges. Halve and stone the olives and slice the sun-dried tomatoes. Add the tomatoes, olives and sun-dried tomatoes to the pasta and toss well.

Transfer the pasta mixture to a salad bowl and scatter the pine kernels and Parmesan cheese over the top. Garnish with a fresh basil sprig and serve warm.

SERVES 6

225 g/8 oz dried fusilli

4 tomatoes, peeled

55 g/2 oz black olives

25 g/1 oz sun-dried tomatoes in oil, drained

2 tbsp pine kernels, toasted

2 tbsp freshly grated Parmesan cheese

salt

1 fresh basil sprig, to garnish

pesto vinaigrette

4 tbsp chopped fresh basil

1 garlic clove, very finely chopped

2 tbsp freshly grated Parmesan cheese

4 tbsp olive oil

2 tbsp lemon juice

pepper

PASTA SALAD WITH CHARGRILLED PEPPERS

Put the whole peppers on a baking sheet and place under a preheated grill, turning frequently, for 15 minutes, until charred all over. Remove with tongs and place in a bowl. Cover with crumpled kitchen paper and set aside.

Meanwhile, bring a large saucepan of lightly salted water to the boil. Add the pasta, bring back to the boil and cook for 8–10 minutes, until tender but still firm to the bite.

Combine the oil, lemon juice, pesto and garlic in a bowl, whisking well to mix. Drain the pasta, add it to the pesto mixture while still hot and toss well. Set aside.

When the peppers are cool enough to handle, peel off the skins, then cut open and remove the seeds. Chop the flesh roughly and add to the pasta with the basil. Season to taste with salt and pepper and toss well. Serve at room temperature.

SERVES 4

1 red pepper

1 orange pepper

280 g/10 oz dried conchiglie

5 tbsp extra virgin olive oil

2 tbsp lemon juice

2 tbsp pesto

1 garlic clove, crushed

3 tbsp shredded fresh basil leaves

salt and pepper

WARM PASTA
SALAD

SERVES 4

225 g/8 oz dried farfalle

6 pieces of sun-dried tomato in
   oil, drained and chopped

4 spring onions, chopped

55 g/2 oz rocket, shredded

½ cucumber, deseeded and diced

2 tbsp freshly grated Parmesan
   cheese

salt and pepper

dressing

4 tbsp olive oil

1 tbsp white wine vinegar

½ tsp caster sugar

1 tsp Dijon mustard

4 fresh basil leaves, finely
   shredded

salt and pepper

To make the dressing, whisk the oil, vinegar, sugar and mustard together in a jug. Season to taste with salt and pepper and stir in the basil.

Bring a large heavy-based saucepan of lightly salted water to the boil. Add the pasta, bring back to the boil and cook for 8–10 minutes, or until tender but still firm to the bite. Drain and transfer to a salad bowl. Add the dressing and toss well.

Add the sun-dried tomatoes, spring onions, rocket and cucumber, season to taste with salt and pepper and toss. Sprinkle with the Parmesan cheese and serve warm.

PASTA & CHICKEN MEDLEY

To make the dressing, whisk the vinegar and oil together well, then season to taste with salt and pepper.

Bring a large saucepan of lightly salted water to the boil. Add the pasta, bring back to the boil and cook for 8–10 minutes, until tender but still firm to the bite. Drain thoroughly, rinse and drain again. Transfer to a bowl and mix in 1 tablespoon of the dressing while hot, then set aside until cold.

Combine the mayonnaise, pesto and soured cream in a bowl, and season to taste with salt and pepper.

Add the chicken, celery, grapes, carrot and the mayonnaise mixture to the pasta, and toss thoroughly. Check the seasoning, adding more salt and pepper if necessary.

Arrange the pasta mixture in a large serving bowl, garnish with the celery leaves and serve.

SERVES 2

125–150 g/4½–5½ oz dried fusilli

2 tbsp mayonnaise

2 tsp pesto

1 tbsp soured cream or natural fromage frais

175 g/6 oz cooked skinless, boneless chicken, cut into strips

1–2 celery sticks, sliced diagonally

125 g/4½ oz black grapes, halved and deseeded

1 large carrot, cut into strips

salt and pepper

celery leaves, to garnish

dressing

1 tbsp white wine vinegar

3 tbsp extra virgin olive oil

salt and pepper

RARE BEEF
PASTA SALAD

Season the steak to taste with salt and pepper, then grill or pan-fry for 4 minutes on each side. Leave to rest for 5 minutes, then, using a sharp knife, slice the steak thinly across the grain and reserve until required.

Meanwhile, bring a large pan of lightly salted water to the boil over a medium heat. Add the pasta and cook for 8–10 minutes, until tender but still firm to the bite. Drain thoroughly, refresh in cold water and drain again. Toss the pasta in the oil.

Mix the lime juice, fish sauce and honey together in a small pan and cook over a medium heat for about 2 minutes.

Add the spring onions, cucumber, tomato wedges and mint to the pan, then add the steak and mix well. Season with salt to taste.

Transfer the pasta to a large warmed serving dish and top with the steak mixture. Serve just warm or leave to cool completely.

SERVES 4

450 g/1 lb rump or sirloin steak in 1 piece

450 g/1 lb dried fusilli

4 tbsp olive oil

2 tbsp lime juice

2 tbsp Thai fish sauce

2 tsp clear honey

4 spring onions, sliced

1 cucumber, peeled and cut into 2.5-cm/1-inch chunks

3 tomatoes, cut into wedges

3 tsp finely chopped fresh mint

salt and pepper

SPICY SAUSAGE
SALAD

SERVES 4

125 g/4½ oz dried conchiglie

2 tbsp olive oil

1 medium onion, chopped

2 garlic cloves, very finely chopped

1 small yellow pepper, deseeded
   and cut into matchsticks

175 g/6 oz spicy pork sausage,
   such as chorizo, Italian
   pepperoni or salami, skinned
   and sliced

2 tbsp red wine

1 tbsp red wine vinegar

125 g/4½ oz mixed salad leaves

salt

Bring a pan of lightly salted water to the boil over a medium heat.
Add the pasta and cook for 8–10 minutes, or until tender but still
firm to the bite. Drain thoroughly and reserve.

Heat the oil in a pan over a medium heat. Add the onion and
cook until translucent. Stir in the garlic, yellow pepper and
sausage and cook for about 3–4 minutes, stirring once or twice.

Add the wine, vinegar and reserved pasta to the pan, stir and
bring the mixture just to the boil over a medium heat.

Arrange the salad leaves on large serving plates, spoon over
the warm sausage and pasta mixture and serve immediately.

NIÇOISE PASTA SALAD

Bring a large pan of lightly salted water to the boil over a medium heat. Add the pasta and cook for 8–10 minutes, until tender but still firm to the bite. Drain and refresh in cold water.

Bring a small pan of lightly salted water to the boil over a medium heat. Add the green beans and cook for 10–12 minutes, or until tender but still firm to the bite. Drain, refresh in cold water, drain again and reserve.

Put the anchovies in a shallow bowl, pour over the milk and leave to stand for 10 minutes. Meanwhile, tear the lettuces into large pieces. Blanch the tomatoes in boiling water for 1–2 minutes, then drain, skin and roughly chop the flesh. Shell the eggs and cut into quarters. Flake the tuna into large chunks.

Drain the anchovies and the pasta. Put all the salad ingredients into a large bowl and gently mix together.

To make the vinaigrette dressing, beat together the oil, vinegar and mustard and season to taste with salt and pepper. Chill in the refrigerator until required. Just before serving, pour the vinaigrette dressing over the salad.

SERVES 4

350 g/12 oz dried conchiglie

115 g/4 oz green beans

50 g/1¾ oz canned anchovy fillets, drained

2 tbsp milk

2 small crisp lettuces

3 large beef tomatoes

4 hard-boiled eggs

225 g/8 oz canned tuna, drained

115 g/4 oz stoned black olives

salt

vinaigrette dressing

3 tbsp extra virgin olive oil

2 tbsp white wine vinegar

1 tsp wholegrain mustard

salt and pepper

PASTA SALAD WITH MELON & PRAWNS

Bring a large pan of salted water to the boil. Add the pasta, bring back to the boil and cook for 8–10 minutes, until tender but still firm to the bite. Drain, toss with 1 tablespoon of the oil and leave to cool.

Meanwhile, peel and devein the prawns, then place them in a large bowl. Halve both the melons and scoop out the seeds with a spoon. Using a melon baller or teaspoon, scoop out balls of the flesh and add them to the prawns.

Whisk together the remaining oil, the vinegar, mustard, sugar, parsley and chopped basil in a small bowl. Season to taste with salt and pepper. Add the cooled pasta to the prawn and melon mixture and toss lightly to mix, then pour in the dressing and toss again. Cover with clingfilm and chill in the refrigerator for 30 minutes.

Make a bed of shredded lettuce on a serving plate. Spoon the pasta salad on top, garnish with basil sprigs and serve.

SERVES 6

225 g/8 oz dried green fusilli

5 tbsp extra virgin olive oil

450 g/1 lb cooked prawns

1 Charentais melon

1 Galia melon

1 tbsp red wine vinegar

1 tsp Dijon mustard

pinch of caster sugar

1 tbsp chopped fresh flat-leaf parsley

1 tbsp chopped fresh basil, plus extra sprigs to garnish

1 oakleaf or quattro stagioni lettuce, shredded

salt and pepper

MEAT & POULTRY

SPAGHETTI BOLOGNESE

Heat the oil in a large frying pan. Add the onion and cook for 3 minutes. Add the garlic, carrot, celery and pancetta and sauté for 3–4 minutes, or until just beginning to brown.

Add the beef and cook over a high heat for another 3 minutes or until all of the meat is browned. Stir in the tomatoes, oregano and wine and bring to the boil. Reduce the heat and leave to simmer for about 45 minutes.

Stir in the tomato purée and season to taste with salt and pepper.

Bring a large saucepan of lightly salted water to the boil. Add the pasta, bring back to the boil and cook for 8–10 minutes, until tender but still firm to the bite. Drain thoroughly.

Transfer the spaghetti to a serving plate and pour over the bolognese sauce. Toss to mix well, garnish with parsley and serve hot.

SERVES 4

1 tbsp olive oil

1 onion, finely chopped

2 garlic cloves, chopped

1 carrot, chopped

1 celery stick, chopped

50 g/1¾ oz pancetta or streaky bacon, diced

350 g/12 oz fresh lean beef mince

400 g/14 oz canned chopped tomatoes

2 tsp dried oregano

125 ml/4 fl oz red wine

2 tbsp tomato purée

350 g/12 oz dried spaghetti

salt and pepper

chopped fresh parsley, to garnish

SPAGHETTI WITH MEATBALLS

Place the potato in a small pan, add cold water to cover and a pinch of salt and bring to the boil. Cook for 10–15 minutes, until tender, then drain. Either mash thoroughly with a potato masher or fork, or pass through a potato ricer.

Combine the potato, beef, onion, egg and parsley in a bowl and season to taste with salt and pepper. Spread out the flour on a plate. With dampened hands, shape the meat mixture into walnut-sized balls and roll in the flour. Shake off any excess.

Heat the oil in a heavy-based frying pan, add the meatballs and cook over a medium heat, stirring and turning frequently, for 8–10 minutes, until golden all over.

Add the passata and tomato purée and cook for a further 10 minutes, until the sauce is reduced and thickened.

Meanwhile, bring a large saucepan of lightly salted water to the boil. Add the pasta, bring back to the boil and cook for 8–10 minutes, or until tender but still firm to the bite.

Drain well and add to the meatball sauce, tossing well to coat. Transfer to a warmed serving dish, garnish with the basil and serve immediately with freshly grated Parmesan cheese.

SERVES 6

1 potato, diced

400 g/14 oz fresh beef mince

1 onion, finely chopped

1 egg

4 tbsp chopped fresh flat-leaf parsley

plain flour, for dusting

5 tbsp olive oil

400 ml/14 fl oz passata

2 tbsp tomato purée

400 g/14 oz dried spaghetti

salt and pepper

shredded fresh basil, to garnish

freshly grated Parmesan cheese, to serve

TAGLIATELLE & MEATBALLS IN RED WINE SAUCE

SERVES 4

150 g/5½ oz white breadcrumbs

150 ml/5 fl oz milk

12 shallots, chopped

450 g/1 lb fresh beef mince

1 tsp paprika

450 g/1 lb dried tagliatelle

salt and pepper

1 fresh basil sprig, to garnish

italian red wine sauce

25 g/1 oz butter

8 tbsp olive oil

225 g/8 oz oyster mushrooms

25 g/1 oz wholemeal flour

200 ml/7 fl oz beef stock

150 ml/5 fl oz red wine

4 tomatoes, peeled and chopped

1 tbsp tomato purée

1 tsp brown sugar

1 tbsp finely chopped fresh basil

salt and pepper

To make the meatballs, put the breadcrumbs into a bowl and pour over the milk. Soak for 30 minutes.

To make the sauce, heat half the butter and half the oil in a saucepan over a low heat. Slice the mushrooms, add to the pan and cook for 4 minutes. Stir in the flour and cook for 2 minutes. Add the stock and wine and simmer for 15 minutes. Add the tomatoes, tomato purée, sugar and basil. Season to taste with salt and pepper and cook for 30 minutes.

Preheat the oven to 180°C/350°F/Gas Mark 4. Mix the shallots, beef and paprika with the soaked breadcrumbs and season to taste with salt and pepper. Shape into 12 meatballs.

Heat the remaining oil and remaining butter in a large frying pan. Add the meatballs and cook until browned. Transfer to a large casserole dish and pour over the sauce. Bake in the preheated oven for 30 minutes.

Bring a large pan of lightly salted water to the boil over a medium heat. Add the pasta and cook for 8–10 minutes, or until tender but still firm to the bite. Drain and transfer to a serving dish. Remove the casserole from the oven and pour the meatballs and sauce onto the pasta. Garnish with a basil sprig and serve.

SPAGHETTI ALLA CARBONARA

Bring a large heavy-based saucepan of lightly salted water to the boil. Add the pasta, return to the boil and cook for 8–10 minutes, or until tender but still firm to the bite.

Meanwhile, heat the oil in a heavy-based frying pan. Add the pancetta and cook over a medium heat, stirring frequently, for 8–10 minutes.

Beat the eggs with the cream in a small bowl and season to taste with salt and pepper. Drain the pasta and return it to the saucepan. Tip in the contents of the frying pan, then add the egg mixture and half the Parmesan cheese. Stir well, then transfer to a warmed serving dish. Serve immediately, sprinkled with the remaining cheese.

SERVES 4

450 g/1 lb dried spaghetti

1 tbsp olive oil

225 g/8 oz rindless pancetta or streaky bacon, chopped

4 eggs

5 tbsp single cream

2 tbsp freshly grated Parmesan cheese

salt and pepper

PASTA WITH BACON & TOMATOES

Blanch the tomatoes in boiling water. Drain, peel and deseed the tomatoes, then roughly chop the flesh.

Using a sharp knife, chop the bacon into small dice. Melt the butter in a saucepan. Add the bacon and cook until it is golden.

Add the onion and garlic and cook over a medium heat for 5–7 minutes, until just softened.

Add the tomatoes and oregano to the saucepan and then season to taste with salt and pepper. Lower the heat and simmer for 10–12 minutes.

Bring a large pan of lightly salted water to the boil. Add the pasta and cook for 8–10 minutes, or until just tender but still firm to the bite. Drain the pasta and transfer to a warmed serving dish or bowl.

Spoon the bacon and tomato sauce over the pasta, toss to coat and serve with the pecorino cheese.

SERVES 4

900 g/2 lb small, sweet tomatoes

6 rashers rindless smoked bacon

55 g/2 oz butter

1 onion, chopped

1 garlic clove, crushed

4 fresh oregano sprigs, finely chopped

450 g/1 lb dried orecchiette

salt and pepper

freshly grated pecorino cheese, to serve

LINGUINE WITH BACON & OLIVES

SERVES 4

3 tbsp olive oil

2 onions, thinly sliced

2 garlic cloves, finely chopped

175 g/6 oz rindless lean bacon, diced

225 g/8 oz mushrooms, sliced

5 canned anchovy fillets, drained

6 black olives, stoned and halved

450 g/1 lb dried linguine

25 g/1 oz freshly grated Parmesan cheese

salt and pepper

Heat the oil in a large frying pan. Add the onions, garlic and bacon and cook over a low heat, stirring occasionally, until the onions are softened. Stir in the mushrooms, anchovies and olives, then season to taste with salt, if necessary, and pepper. Simmer for 5 minutes.

Meanwhile, bring a large heavy-based saucepan of lightly salted water to the boil. Add the pasta, return to the boil and cook for 8–10 minutes, or until tender but still firm to the bite.

Drain the pasta and transfer to a warmed serving dish. Spoon the sauce on top, toss lightly and sprinkle with the Parmesan cheese. Serve immediately.

PENNE WITH HAM, TOMATO & CHILLI SAUCE

Put the oil and 1 tablespoon of the butter in a large saucepan over a medium–low heat. Add the onion and cook for 10 minutes, or until soft and golden. Add the ham and cook for 5 minutes, or until lightly browned. Stir in the garlic, chilli and tomatoes. Season to taste with salt and pepper. Bring to the boil, then simmer over a medium–low heat for 30–40 minutes, until thickened.

Meanwhile, bring a large heavy-based saucepan of lightly salted water to the boil. Add the pasta, return to the boil and cook for 8–10 minutes, or until tender but still firm to the bite. Drain and transfer to a warmed serving dish.

Pour the sauce over the pasta. Add the parsley, Parmesan cheese and the remaining butter. Toss well to mix and serve immediately.

SERVES 4

1 tbsp olive oil

2 tbsp butter

1 onion, finely chopped

150 g/5½ oz ham, diced

2 garlic cloves, very finely chopped

1 fresh red chilli, deseeded and finely chopped

800 g/1 lb 12 oz canned chopped tomatoes

450 g/1 lb dried penne

2 tbsp chopped fresh flat-leaf parsley

6 tbsp freshly grated Parmesan cheese

salt and pepper

SAFFRON LINGUINE

Bring a large heavy-based saucepan of lightly salted water to the boil. Add the pasta, return to the boil and cook for 8–10 minutes, or until tender but still firm to the bite.

Meanwhile, place the saffron in a separate heavy-based saucepan and add the water. Bring to the boil, then remove from the heat and leave to stand for 5 minutes.

Stir the ham, cream and Parmesan cheese into the saffron and return the saucepan to the heat. Season to taste with salt and pepper and heat through gently, stirring constantly, until simmering. Remove the saucepan from the heat and beat in the egg yolks. Drain the pasta and transfer to a warmed serving dish. Add the saffron sauce, toss well and serve immediately.

SERVES 4

350 g/12 oz dried linguine

pinch of saffron threads

2 tbsp water

140 g/5 oz cooked ham, cut into strips

175 ml/6 fl oz double cream

55 g/2 oz freshly grated Parmesan cheese

2 egg yolks

salt and pepper

FARFALLE WITH GORGONZOLA & HAM

SERVES 4

225 ml/8 fl oz crème fraîche

225 g/8 oz chestnut mushrooms, quartered

400 g/14 oz dried farfalle

85 g/3 oz Gorgonzola cheese, crumbled

1 tbsp chopped fresh flat-leaf parsley, plus extra sprigs to garnish

175 g/6 oz cooked ham, diced

salt and pepper

Pour the crème fraîche into a saucepan, add the mushrooms and season to taste with salt and pepper. Bring to just below the boil, then lower the heat and simmer very gently, stirring occasionally, for 8–10 minutes, until thickened.

Meanwhile, bring a large pan of lightly salted water to the boil. Add the pasta, bring back to the boil and cook for 8–10 minutes, until tender but still firm to the bite.

Remove the pan containing the mushroom mixture from the heat and stir in the Gorgonzola cheese until it has melted. Return the pan to a very low heat and stir in the chopped parsley and ham.

Drain the pasta and add it to the sauce. Toss lightly, then divide between individual warmed plates, garnish with parsley sprigs and serve.

PEPPERONI
PASTA

Heat 2 tablespoons of the oil in a large heavy-based frying pan. Add the onion and cook over a low heat, stirring occasionally, for 5 minutes, or until softened. Add the red and orange peppers, tomatoes and their can juices, sun-dried tomato paste and paprika and bring to the boil.

Add the pepperoni and parsley and season to taste with salt and pepper. Stir well, bring to the boil, then reduce the heat and simmer for 10–15 minutes.

Meanwhile, bring a large heavy-based saucepan of lightly salted water to the boil. Add the pasta, return to the boil and cook for 8–10 minutes, or until tender but still firm to the bite. Drain well and transfer to a warmed serving dish. Add the remaining olive oil and toss. Add the sauce and toss again. Sprinkle with parsley and serve immediately.

SERVES 4

3 tbsp olive oil

1 onion, chopped

1 red pepper, deseeded and diced

1 orange pepper, deseeded and diced

800 g/1 lb 12 oz canned chopped tomatoes

1 tbsp sun-dried tomato paste

1 tsp paprika

225 g/8 oz pepperoni sausage, sliced

2 tbsp chopped fresh flat-leaf parsley, plus extra to garnish

450 g/1 lb dried penne

salt and pepper

RIGATONI WITH CHORIZO & MUSHROOMS

Heat the oil in a frying pan. Add the onion, garlic and celery and cook over a low heat, stirring occasionally, for 5 minutes, until softened.

Meanwhile, bring a large saucepan of lightly salted water to the boil. Add the pasta, bring back to the boil and cook for 8–10 minutes, until tender but still firm to the bite.

While the pasta is cooking, add the chorizo to the frying pan and cook, stirring occasionally, for 5 minutes, until evenly browned. Add the mushrooms and cook, stirring occasionally, for a further 5 minutes. Stir in the coriander and lime juice and season to taste with salt and pepper.

Drain the pasta and return it to the pan. Add the chorizo and mushroom mixture and toss lightly. Divide between individual warmed plates and serve immediately.

SERVES 4

4 tbsp olive oil

1 red onion, chopped

1 garlic clove, chopped

1 celery stick, sliced

400 g/14 oz dried rigatoni

280 g/10 oz chorizo sausage, sliced

225 g/8 oz chestnut mushrooms, halved

1 tbsp chopped fresh coriander

1 tbsp lime juice

salt and pepper

MACARONI WITH SAUSAGE, PEPPERONCINI & OLIVES

SERVES 6

1 tbsp olive oil

1 large onion, finely chopped

2 garlic cloves, very finely chopped

450 g/1 lb pork sausage, peeled and roughly chopped

3 canned pepperoncini, or other hot red peppers, drained and sliced

400 g/14 oz canned chopped tomatoes

2 tsp dried oregano

125 ml/4 fl oz chicken stock or red wine

450 g/1 lb dried macaroni

12–15 stoned black olives, quartered

75 g/2¾ oz freshly grated cheese, such as Cheddar or Gruyère

salt and pepper

Heat the oil in a large frying pan over a medium heat. Add the onion and cook for 5 minutes, until softened. Add the garlic and cook for a few seconds, until just beginning to colour. Add the sausage and cook until evenly browned.

Stir in the pepperoncini, tomatoes, oregano and stock. Season to taste with salt and pepper. Bring to the boil, then simmer over a medium heat for 10 minutes, stirring occasionally.

Meanwhile, bring a large saucepan of lightly salted water to the boil. Add the pasta, bring back to the boil and cook for 8–10 minutes, or until tender but still firm to the bite. Drain and transfer to a warmed serving dish.

Add the olives and half the cheese to the sauce, then stir until the cheese has melted.

Pour the sauce over the pasta. Toss well to mix. Sprinkle with the remaining cheese and serve immediately.

PASTA & PORK IN CREAM SAUCE

To make the red wine sauce, heat the oil in a small heavy-based saucepan, add the onion and cook until translucent. Stir in the tomato purée, red wine and oregano. Heat gently to reduce and set aside.

Pound the slices of pork between 2 sheets of clingfilm until wafer thin, then cut into strips. Heat the oil in a frying pan, add the pork and cook for 5 minutes. Add the mushrooms and cook for a further 2 minutes. Strain and pour over the red wine sauce. Reduce the heat and simmer for 20 minutes.

Meanwhile, bring a large heavy-based saucepan of lightly salted water to the boil. Add the lemon juice, saffron and pasta, return to the boil and cook for 8–10 minutes, or until tender but still firm to the bite. Drain the pasta thoroughly, return to the saucepan and keep warm.

Stir the cream into the saucepan with the pork and heat for a few minutes.

Boil the quail eggs for 3 minutes, cool them in cold water and remove the shells.Transfer the pasta to a large warmed serving plate, top with the pork and the sauce and garnish with the eggs. Serve immediately.

SERVES 4

450 g/1 lb pork fillet, thinly sliced

4 tbsp olive oil

225 g/8 oz button mushrooms, sliced

1 tbsp lemon juice

pinch of saffron threads

350 g/12 oz dried orecchiette

4 tbsp double cream

12 quail eggs

salt

red wine sauce

1 tbsp olive oil

1 onion, chopped

1 tbsp tomato purée

200 ml/7 fl oz red wine

1 tsp finely chopped fresh oregano

TAGLIATELLE WITH SPRING LAMB

Using a sharp knife, cut small pockets all over the lamb, then insert a garlic slice and a few rosemary leaves in each one. Heat 2 tablespoons of the oil in a large heavy-based frying pan. Add the lamb and cook over a medium heat, turning occasionally, for 25–30 minutes, until tender and cooked to your liking.

Meanwhile, chop the remaining rosemary and place in a mortar. Add the remaining oil and pound with a pestle. Season to taste with salt and pepper and set aside.

Remove the lamb from the heat, cover with foil and leave to stand. Bring a large pan of lightly salted water to the boil. Add the pasta, bring back to the boil and cook for 8–10 minutes, until tender but still firm to the bite.

Meanwhile, melt the butter in another pan. Add the mushrooms and cook over a medium–low heat, stirring occasionally, for 5–8 minutes, until tender.

Drain the pasta, return it to the pan and toss with half the rosemary oil. Uncover the lamb and cut it into slices. Divide the tagliatelle between individual warmed plates, season with pepper and top with the lamb and mushrooms. Drizzle with the remaining rosemary oil, sprinkle with the pecorino cheese and serve immediately.

SERVES 4

750 g/1 lb 10 oz boneless lean lamb in a single piece

6 garlic cloves, thinly sliced

6–8 fresh rosemary sprigs

125 ml/4 fl oz olive oil

400 g/14 oz dried tagliatelle

55 g/2 oz butter

175 g/6 oz button mushrooms

salt and pepper

fresh pecorino cheese shavings, to serve

SPAGHETTI WITH PARSLEY CHICKEN

SERVES 4

1 tbsp olive oil

thinly pared rind of 1 lemon, cut into julienne strips

1 tsp finely chopped fresh ginger

1 tsp sugar

225 ml/8 fl oz chicken stock

250 g/9 oz dried spaghetti

55 g/2 oz butter

225 g/8 oz skinless, boneless chicken breasts, diced

1 red onion, finely chopped

leaves from 2 bunches of flat-leaf parsley

salt

Heat the oil in a heavy-based saucepan. Add the lemon rind and cook over a low heat, stirring frequently, for 5 minutes. Stir in the ginger and sugar, season to taste with salt and cook, stirring constantly, for a further 2 minutes. Pour in the stock, bring to the boil, then cook for 5 minutes, or until the liquid has reduced by half.

Meanwhile, bring a large heavy-based saucepan of lightly salted water to the boil. Add the pasta, return to the boil and cook for 8–10 minutes, or until tender but still firm to the bite.

Melt half the butter in a frying pan. Add the chicken and onion and cook, stirring frequently, for 5 minutes, or until the chicken is lightly browned all over. Stir in the lemon and ginger mixture and cook for 1 minute. Stir in the parsley leaves and cook, stirring constantly, for a further 3 minutes.

Drain the pasta and transfer to a warmed serving dish, then add the remaining butter and toss well. Add the chicken sauce, toss again and serve.

PAPPARDELLE
WITH CHICKEN
& PORCINI

Place the porcini in a small bowl, add the hot water and leave to soak for 20 minutes. Meanwhile, place the tomatoes and their can juices in a heavy-based saucepan and break them up with a wooden spoon, then stir in the chilli. Bring to the boil, reduce the heat and simmer, stirring occasionally, for 30 minutes, or until reduced.

Remove the mushrooms from their soaking liquid with a slotted spoon, reserving the liquid. Strain the liquid through a coffee filter paper or muslin-lined sieve into the tomatoes and simmer for a further 15 minutes.

Meanwhile, heat 2 tablespoons of the oil in a heavy-based frying pan. Add the chicken and cook, stirring frequently, until golden brown all over and tender. Stir in the mushrooms and garlic and cook for a further 5 minutes.

Meanwhile, bring a large heavy-based saucepan of lightly salted water to the boil. Add the pasta, return to the boil and cook for 8–10 minutes, or until tender but still firm to the bite. Drain well, transfer to a warmed serving dish, drizzle with the remaining oil and toss lightly. Stir the chicken mixture into the tomato sauce, season to taste with salt and pepper and spoon on top of the pasta. Toss lightly, sprinkle with parsley and serve immediately.

SERVES 4

40 g/1½ oz dried porcini
  mushrooms

175 ml/6 fl oz hot water

800 g/1 lb 12 oz canned chopped
  tomatoes

1 fresh red chilli, deseeded and
  finely chopped

3 tbsp olive oil

350 g/12 oz skinless, boneless
  chicken, cut into thin strips

2 garlic cloves, finely chopped

350 g/12 oz dried pappardelle

salt and pepper

2 tbsp chopped fresh flat-leaf
  parsley, to garnish

PENNE WITH CHICKEN & FETA

Heat the oil in a heavy-based frying pan. Add the chicken and cook over a medium heat, stirring frequently, for 5–8 minutes, or until golden all over and cooked through. Add the spring onions and cook for 2 minutes. Stir the feta cheese into the frying pan with half the chives and season to taste with salt and pepper.

Meanwhile, bring a large heavy-based saucepan of lightly salted water to the boil. Add the pasta, return to the boil and cook for 8–10 minutes, or until tender but still firm to the bite. Drain well, then transfer to a warmed serving dish.

Spoon the chicken mixture onto the pasta, toss lightly and serve immediately, garnished with the remaining chives.

SERVES 4

2 tbsp olive oil

450 g/1 lb skinless, boneless chicken breasts, cut into thin strips

6 spring onions, chopped

225 g/8 oz feta cheese, diced

4 tbsp snipped fresh chives

450 g/1 lb dried penne

salt and pepper

PENNE WITH CHICKEN & ROCKET

SERVES 4

25 g/1 oz butter

2 carrots, cut into thin batons

1 small onion, finely chopped

225 g/8 oz skinless, boneless
   chicken breasts, diced

225 g/8 oz mushrooms, quartered

125 ml/4 fl oz dry white wine

125 ml/4 fl oz chicken stock

2 garlic cloves, finely chopped

2 tbsp cornflour

4 tbsp water

2 tbsp single cream

125 ml/4 fl oz natural yogurt

2 tsp fresh thyme leaves,
   plus extra sprigs to garnish

115 g/4 oz rocket

350 g/12 oz dried penne

salt and pepper

Melt the butter in a heavy-based frying pan. Add the carrots and cook over a medium heat, stirring frequently, for 2 minutes. Add the onion, chicken, mushrooms, wine, stock and garlic and season to taste with salt and pepper. Mix the cornflour and water together in a bowl until a smooth paste forms, then stir in the cream and yogurt. Stir the cornflour mixture into the frying pan with the thyme, cover and leave to simmer for 5 minutes. Place the rocket on top of the chicken, but do not stir in, cover and cook for 5 minutes, or until the chicken is tender.

Strain the cooking liquid into a saucepan, then transfer the chicken and vegetables to a dish and keep warm. Heat the cooking liquid, whisking occasionally, for 10 minutes, or until reduced and thickened.

Meanwhile, bring a large heavy-based saucepan of lightly salted water to the boil. Add the pasta, return to the boil and cook for 8–10 minutes, or until tender but still firm to the bite. Return the chicken and vegetables to the thickened cooking liquid and stir to coat.

Drain the pasta well, transfer to a warmed serving dish and spoon the chicken and vegetable mixture on top. Garnish with thyme sprigs and serve immediately.

PASTA WITH TWO SAUCES

To make the tomato sauce, heat the oil in a pan over a medium heat. Add the onion and cook until translucent. Add the garlic and cook for 1 minute. Stir in the tomatoes, parsley, oregano, bay leaves, tomato purée and sugar. Season to taste with salt and pepper, bring to the boil and simmer, uncovered, for 15–20 minutes, until reduced by half. Remove the pan from the heat and discard the bay leaves.

To make the chicken sauce, melt the butter in a frying pan over a medium heat. Add the chicken and almonds and cook for 5–6 minutes, or until the chicken is cooked through.

Meanwhile, bring the cream to the boil in a small pan over a low heat and boil for about 10 minutes, until reduced by almost half. Pour the cream over the chicken and almonds, stir and season to taste with salt and pepper. Reserve and keep warm.

Bring a large pan of lightly salted water to the boil over a medium heat. Add the pasta and cook for about 8–10 minutes, or until tender but still firm to the bite. Drain and transfer to a warmed serving dish. Spoon over the tomato sauce and arrange the chicken sauce on top. Garnish with fresh basil leaves and serve.

SERVES 4

2 tbsp olive oil

1 small onion, chopped

1 garlic clove, chopped

400 g/14 oz canned chopped tomatoes

2 tbsp chopped fresh parsley

1 tsp dried oregano

2 bay leaves

2 tbsp tomato purée

1 tsp sugar

55 g/2 oz unsalted butter

400 g/14 oz skinless, boneless chicken breasts, cut into thin slices

85 g/3 oz blanched almonds

300 ml/10 fl oz double cream

350 g/12 oz dried green tagliatelle

salt and pepper

fresh basil leaves, to garnish

CHICKEN & MUSHROOM TAGLIATELLE

Put the dried mushrooms in a bowl with the hot water. Leave to soak for 30 minutes until softened. Remove, squeezing excess water back into the bowl. Strain the liquid in a fine-meshed sieve and reserve. Slice the soaked mushrooms, discarding the stems.

Heat the oil in a large frying pan over a medium heat. Add the bacon and chicken, then cook for about 3 minutes. Add the dried and fresh mushrooms, the onion and oregano. Cook for 5–7 minutes, until soft. Pour in the stock and the mushroom liquid. Bring to the boil, stirring. Simmer briskly for about 10 minutes, continuing to stir, until reduced. Add the cream and simmer for 5 minutes, stirring, until beginning to thicken. Season to taste with salt and pepper. Remove the pan from the heat and set aside.

Meanwhile, bring a large saucepan of lightly salted water to the boil. Add the pasta, bring back to the boil and cook for 8–10 minutes, or until tender but still firm to the bite. Drain and transfer to a serving dish. Pour the sauce over the pasta. Add half the Parmesan cheese and mix. Sprinkle with parsley and serve with the remaining Parmesan.

SERVES 4

25 g/1 oz dried shiitake mushrooms

350 ml/12 fl oz hot water

1 tbsp olive oil

6 bacon rashers, chopped

3 skinless, boneless chicken breasts, cut into strips

115 g/4 oz fresh shiitake mushrooms, sliced

1 small onion, finely chopped

1 tsp finely chopped fresh oregano or marjoram

250 ml/9 fl oz chicken stock

300 ml/10 fl oz whipping cream

450 g/1 lb dried tagliatelle

55 g/2 oz freshly grated Parmesan cheese

salt and pepper

chopped fresh flat-leaf parsley, to garnish

FARFALLE WITH CHICKEN & BROCCOLI

SERVES 4

4 tbsp olive oil

5 tbsp butter

3 garlic cloves, very finely
chopped

450 g/1 lb skinless, boneless
chicken breasts, diced

¼ tsp dried chilli flakes

450 g/1 lb small broccoli florets

300 g/10½ oz dried farfalle

175 g/6 oz bottled roasted red
peppers, drained and diced

250 ml/9 fl oz chicken stock

salt and pepper

Bring a large pan of salted water to the boil. Meanwhile, heat the
oil and butter in a large frying pan over a medium–low heat. Cook
the garlic until just beginning to colour.

Add the diced chicken, increase the heat to medium and cook
for 4–5 minutes, until the chicken is no longer pink. Add the
chilli flakes and season to taste with salt and pepper. Remove
from the heat.

Plunge the broccoli into the boiling water and cook for
2 minutes. Remove with a slotted spoon and set aside. Bring the
water back to the boil. Add the pasta and cook for 8–10 minutes,
or until tender but still firm to the bite. Drain and add to the
chicken mixture in the frying pan. Add the broccoli and roasted
peppers. Pour in the stock. Simmer briskly over a medium–high
heat, stirring frequently, until most of the liquid has been
absorbed.

Transfer to warmed dishes and serve.

FETTUCCINE WITH CHICKEN & BASIL PESTO

To make the pesto, put the basil, olive oil, pine kernels, garlic and a generous pinch of salt in a food processor or blender. Process the ingredients until smooth. Scrape the mixture into a bowl and stir in the cheeses.

Heat the vegetable oil in a frying pan over a medium heat. Cook the chicken breasts, turning once, for 8–10 minutes, until the juices are no longer pink. Cut into small cubes.

Meanwhile, bring a large saucepan of lightly salted water to the boil. Add the pasta, bring back to the boil and cook for 8–10 minutes, or until tender but still firm to the bite. Drain and transfer to a warmed serving dish. Add the chicken and pesto, then season to taste with pepper. Toss well to mix.

Garnish with a sprig of basil and serve warm.

SERVES 4

2 tbsp vegetable oil

4 skinless, boneless chicken breasts

350 g/12 oz dried fettuccine

salt and pepper

sprig of fresh basil, to garnish

pesto

100 g/3½ oz shredded fresh basil

125 ml/4 fl oz extra virgin olive oil

3 tbsp pine kernels

3 garlic cloves, crushed

55 g/2 oz freshly grated Parmesan cheese

2 tbsp freshly grated pecorino cheese

salt

FETTUCCINE WITH CHICKEN & ONION CREAM SAUCE

Heat the oil and butter with the garlic in a large frying pan over a medium–low heat. Cook the garlic until just beginning to colour. Add the chicken and increase the heat to medium. Cook for 4–5 minutes on each side, until the juices are no longer pink. Season to taste with salt and pepper. Remove from the heat. Remove the chicken from the pan, leaving the oil in the pan. Slice the chicken diagonally into thin strips and set aside.

Reheat the oil in the pan. Add the onion and gently cook for 5 minutes until soft. Add the crumbled stock cube and the water. Bring to the boil, then simmer over a medium–low heat for 10 minutes. Stir in the cream, milk, spring onions and Parmesan cheese. Simmer until heated through and slightly thickened.

Meanwhile, bring a large saucepan of lightly salted water to the boil. Add the pasta, bring back to the boil and cook for 8–10 minutes, or until tender but still firm to the bite. Drain and transfer to a warmed serving dish. Layer the chicken slices over the pasta. Pour over the sauce, garnish with parsley and serve.

SERVES 4

1 tbsp olive oil

2 tbsp butter

1 garlic clove, very finely chopped

4 skinless, boneless chicken breasts

1 onion, finely chopped

1 chicken stock cube, crumbled

125 ml/4 fl oz water

300 ml/10 fl oz double cream

175 ml/6 fl oz milk

6 spring onions, green part included, sliced diagonally

35 g/1¼ oz freshly grated Parmesan cheese

450 g/1 lb dried fettuccine

salt and pepper

chopped fresh flat-leaf parsley, to garnish

PENNE WITH TURKEY MEATBALLS

SERVES 4

350 g/12 oz fresh turkey mince

1 small garlic clove, finely chopped

2 tbsp finely chopped fresh
  parsley

1 egg, lightly beaten

plain flour, for dusting

3 tbsp olive oil

1 onion, finely chopped

1 celery stick, finely chopped

1 carrot, finely chopped

400 ml/14 fl oz passata

1 fresh rosemary sprig

1 bay leaf

350 g/12 oz dried penne

salt and pepper

freshly grated Parmesan cheese,
  to serve

Put the turkey, garlic and parsley in a bowl and mix well. Stir in the egg and season to taste with salt and pepper. Dust your hands lightly with flour and shape the mixture into walnut-sized balls between your palms. Lightly dust each meatball with flour.

Heat the oil in a saucepan. Add the onion, celery and carrot and cook over a low heat, stirring occasionally, for 5 minutes, until softened. Increase the heat to medium, add the meatballs and cook, turning frequently, for 8–10 minutes, until golden brown all over.

Pour in the passata, add the rosemary and bay leaf, season to taste with salt and pepper and bring to the boil. Lower the heat, cover and simmer gently, stirring occasionally, for 40–45 minutes. Remove and discard the herbs.

Shortly before the meatballs are ready, bring a large pan of lightly salted water to the boil. Add the pasta, bring back to the boil and cook for 8–10 minutes, until tender but still firm to the bite. Drain and add to the pan with the meatballs. Stir gently and heat through briefly, then spoon into individual warmed dishes. Sprinkle generously with Parmesan cheese and serve immediately.

FETTUCCINE WITH DUCK SAUCE

Heat half the oil in a frying pan. Add the duck and cook over a medium heat, turning frequently, for 8–10 minutes, until golden brown. Using a slotted spoon, transfer to a large saucepan.

Wipe out the frying pan with kitchen paper, then add the remaining oil. Add the shallot, leek, garlic, celery, carrot and pancetta and cook over a low heat, stirring, for 10 minutes. Using a slotted spoon, transfer the mixture to the pan with the duck and stir in the parsley. Add the bay leaf and season to taste with salt and pepper. Pour in the wine and cook over a high heat, stirring occasionally, until reduced by half. Add the tomatoes, tomato purée and sugar and cook for a further 5 minutes. Pour in just enough water to cover and bring to the boil. Lower the heat, cover and simmer gently for 1 hour, until the duck is cooked through and tender.

Remove the saucepan from the heat and transfer the duck to a chopping board. Skim off the fat from the surface of the sauce and discard the bay leaf. Remove and discard the skin from the duck and cut the meat off the bones, then dice. Return the duck meat to the pan and keep warm.

Bring a large pan of salted water to the boil. Add the pasta, return to the boil and cook for 8–10 minutes, until tender but still firm to the bite. Drain and place in a serving dish. Adjust the seasoning of the sauce, if necessary, then spoon it on top of the pasta. Sprinkle generously with Parmesan and serve.

SERVES 4

4 tbsp olive oil

4 duck legs

1 shallot, finely chopped

1 leek, white part only, finely chopped

1 garlic clove, finely chopped

1 celery stick, finely chopped

1 carrot, finely chopped

4 pancetta or bacon slices, diced

1 tbsp finely chopped fresh flat-leaf parsley

1 bay leaf

5 tbsp dry white wine

400 g/14 oz canned chopped tomatoes

2 tbsp tomato purée

pinch of sugar

450 g/1 lb dried fettuccine

salt and pepper

freshly grated Parmesan cheese, to serve

FISH & SEAFOOD

SPAGHETTI ALLA PUTTANESCA

Heat the oil in a heavy-based frying pan. Add the garlic and cook over a low heat, stirring frequently, for 2 minutes. Add the anchovies and mash them to a pulp with a fork. Add the olives, capers and tomatoes and season to taste with cayenne pepper. Cover and simmer for 25 minutes.

Meanwhile, bring a large heavy-based saucepan of lightly salted water to the boil. Add the pasta, return to the boil and cook for 8–10 minutes, or until tender but still firm to the bite. Drain well and transfer to a warmed serving dish.

Spoon the anchovy sauce into the dish and toss the pasta, using 2 large forks. Garnish with the chopped parsley and serve immediately.

SERVES 4

3 tbsp olive oil

2 garlic cloves, finely chopped

10 canned anchovy fillets, drained and chopped

140 g/5 oz black olives, stoned and chopped

1 tbsp capers, drained and rinsed

450 g/1 lb plum tomatoes, peeled, deseeded and chopped

pinch of cayenne pepper

400 g/14 oz dried spaghetti

salt

2 tbsp chopped fresh parsley, to garnish

PENNE WITH SICILIAN SAUCE

Soak the sultanas in a bowl of warm water for about 20 minutes. Drain the sultanas thoroughly.

Preheat the grill, then cook the tomatoes under the hot grill for 10 minutes. Leave to cool slightly, then once cool enough to handle, peel off the skin and dice the flesh. Place the pine kernels on a baking tray and lightly toast under the grill for 2–3 minutes, or until golden brown.

Place the tomatoes, pine kernels and sultanas in a small saucepan and heat gently. Add the anchovies and tomato purée, and cook the sauce over a low heat for a further 2–3 minutes, or until hot.

Meanwhile, bring a large heavy-based saucepan of lightly salted water to the boil. Add the pasta, return to the boil and cook for 8–10 minutes, or until tender but still firm to the bite. Drain thoroughly, then transfer the pasta to a serving plate and serve with the Sicilian sauce.

SERVES 4

50 g/1¾ oz sultanas

450 g/1 lb tomatoes, halved

25 g/1 oz pine kernels

50 g/1¾ oz canned anchovies, drained and halved lengthways

2 tbsp tomato purée

350 g/12 oz dried penne

salt

SPINACH & ANCHOVY PASTA

SERVES 4

900 g/2 lb fresh, young spinach
  leaves

400 g/14 oz dried fettuccine

5 tbsp olive oil

3 tbsp pine kernels

3 garlic cloves, crushed

8 canned anchovy fillets, drained
  and chopped

salt

Trim off any tough spinach stalks. Rinse the spinach leaves under cold running water and place them in a large saucepan with only the water that is clinging to them after washing. Cover and cook over a high heat, shaking the saucepan from time to time, until the spinach has wilted, but retains its colour. Drain well, reserve and keep warm.

Bring a large heavy-based saucepan of lightly salted water to the boil. Add the pasta, return to the boil and cook for 8–10 minutes, or until tender but still firm to the bite.

Heat 4 tablespoons of the oil in a separate saucepan. Add the pine kernels and cook until golden. Remove the pine kernels from the saucepan and reserve until required.

Add the garlic to the saucepan and cook until golden. Add the anchovies and stir in the spinach. Cook, stirring, for 2–3 minutes, until heated through. Return the pine kernels to the saucepan.

Drain the pasta, toss in the remaining oil and transfer to a warmed serving dish. Spoon the anchovy and spinach sauce over the pasta, toss lightly and serve immediately.

SPAGHETTI WITH TUNA & PARSLEY

Bring a large heavy-based saucepan of lightly salted water to the boil. Add the spaghetti, return to the boil and cook for 8–10 minutes, or until tender but still firm to the bite. Drain the spaghetti in a colander and return to the saucepan. Add the butter, toss thoroughly to coat and keep warm until required.

Flake the tuna into smaller pieces using 2 forks. Place the tuna in a food processor or blender with the anchovies, oil and parsley and process until the sauce is smooth. Pour in the crème fraîche and process for a few seconds to blend. Taste the sauce and season with salt and pepper, if necessary.

Shake the saucepan of spaghetti over a medium heat for a few minutes, or until it is thoroughly warmed.

Pour the sauce over the spaghetti and toss quickly, using 2 forks. Serve immediately.

SERVES 4

500 g/1 lb 2 oz dried spaghetti

25 g/1 oz butter

200 g/7 oz canned tuna, drained

55 g/2 oz canned anchovies, drained

250 ml/9 fl oz olive oil

1 large bunch of fresh flat-leaf parsley, roughly chopped

150 ml/5 fl oz crème fraîche

salt and pepper

GNOCCHI WITH TUNA, CAPERS & OLIVES

Bring a large saucepan of lightly salted water to the boil. Add the pasta, bring back to the boil and cook for 8–10 minutes, or until tender but still firm to the bite. Drain and return to the pan.

Heat the oil and half the butter in a frying pan over a medium–low heat. Add the garlic and cook for a few seconds until just beginning to colour. Reduce the heat to low. Add the tuna, lemon juice, capers and olives. Stir gently until all the ingredients are heated through.

Transfer the pasta to a warmed serving dish. Pour the tuna mixture over the pasta. Add the parsley and remaining butter. Toss well to mix. Serve immediately.

SERVES 4

350 g/12 oz dried gnocchi pasta

4 tbsp olive oil

4 tbsp butter

3 large garlic cloves, thinly sliced

200 g/7 oz canned tuna, drained and broken into chunks

2 tbsp lemon juice

1 tbsp capers, drained

10–12 black olives, stoned and sliced

salt

2 tbsp chopped fresh flat-leaf parsley, to serve

SPAGHETTINI WITH QUICK TUNA SAUCE

SERVES 4

3 tbsp olive oil

4 tomatoes, peeled, deseeded and
  roughly chopped

115 g/4 oz mushrooms, sliced

1 tbsp shredded fresh basil

400 g/14 oz canned tuna, drained

100 ml/3½ fl oz fish or chicken
  stock

1 garlic clove, finely chopped

2 tsp chopped fresh marjoram

350 g/12 oz dried spaghettini

salt and pepper

115 g/4 oz freshly grated
  Parmesan cheese, to serve

Heat the oil in a large frying pan. Add the tomatoes and cook over a low heat, stirring occasionally, for 15 minutes, or until pulpy. Add the mushrooms and cook, stirring occasionally, for a further 10 minutes. Stir in the basil, tuna, stock, garlic and marjoram and season to taste with salt and pepper. Cook over a low heat for 5 minutes, or until heated through.

Meanwhile, bring a large heavy-based saucepan of lightly salted water to the boil. Add the pasta, return to the boil and cook for 8–10 minutes, or until tender but still firm to the bite.

Drain the pasta well, transfer to a warmed serving dish and spoon over the tuna mixture. Serve with grated Parmesan cheese.

LINGUINE WITH SARDINES

Wash the sardine fillets and pat dry on kitchen paper. Roughly chop them into large pieces and reserve. Trim the fennel bulb, discard the outer leaves and slice very thinly.

Heat 2 tablespoons of the oil in a large frying pan over a medium–high heat and add the garlic and chillies. Cook for 1 minute, then add the fennel slices. Cook, stirring occasionally, for 4–5 minutes, or until softened. Reduce the heat, add the sardine pieces and cook for a further 3–4 minutes.

Meanwhile, bring a large pan of lightly salted water to the boil over a medium heat. Add the pasta and cook for 8–10 minutes, or until tender but still firm to the bite. Drain thoroughly and return to the pan.

Add the lemon rind, lemon juice, pine kernels and parsley to the sardine mixture and toss together. Season to taste with salt and pepper. Add to the pasta with the remaining oil and toss together gently. Transfer to a warmed serving dish and serve immediately.

SERVES 4

8 sardines, filleted

1 fennel bulb

4 tbsp olive oil

3 garlic cloves, sliced

1 tsp crushed chillies

350 g/12 oz dried linguine

½ tsp finely grated lemon rind

1 tbsp lemon juice

2 tbsp pine kernels, toasted

2 tbsp chopped fresh parsley

salt and pepper

FUSILLI WITH SMOKED SALMON & DILL

Bring a large heavy-based saucepan of lightly salted water to the boil. Add the pasta, return to the boil and cook for 8–10 minutes, or until tender but still firm to the bite.

Meanwhile, melt the butter in a heavy-based saucepan. Add the onion and cook over a low heat, stirring occasionally, for 5 minutes, or until softened. Add the wine, bring to the boil and continue boiling until reduced by two thirds. Pour in the cream and season to taste with salt and pepper. Bring to the boil, reduce the heat and simmer for 2 minutes, or until slightly thickened. Cut the smoked salmon into squares and stir into the saucepan with the snipped dill and lemon juice to taste.

Drain the pasta and transfer to a warmed serving dish. Add the smoked salmon mixture, toss well, garnish with dill sprigs and serve immediately.

SERVES 4

450 g/1 lb dried fusilli

55 g/2 oz unsalted butter

1 small onion, finely chopped

6 tbsp dry white wine

425 ml/15 fl oz double cream

225 g/8 oz smoked salmon

2 tbsp snipped fresh dill, plus extra sprigs to garnish

1–2 tbsp lemon juice

salt and pepper

CONCHIGLIE WITH SMOKED SALMON & SOURED CREAM

SERVES 4

450 g/1 lb dried conchiglie

300 ml/10 fl oz soured cream

2 tsp Dijon mustard

4 large spring onions, finely sliced

225 g/8 oz smoked salmon,
   cut into bite-sized pieces

finely grated rind of ½ lemon

salt and pepper

2 tbsp snipped fresh chives,
   to garnish

Bring a large saucepan of lightly salted water to a boil. Add the pasta, bring back to the boil and cook for 8–10 minutes, or until tender but still firm to the bite. Drain and return to the pan.

Add the soured cream, mustard, spring onions, smoked salmon and lemon rind to the pasta. Stir over a low heat until heated through. Season to taste with pepper.

Transfer to a serving dish. Sprinkle with the chives and serve.

FUSILLI WITH SALMON & PRAWNS

Place the salmon in a large heavy-based frying pan. Add a few dill sprigs, pour in the wine and season to taste with salt and pepper. Bring to the boil, then reduce the heat, cover and poach gently for 5 minutes, or until the flesh flakes easily. Remove with a fish slice, reserving the cooking liquid, and leave to cool slightly. Remove and discard the skin and any remaining small bones, then flake the flesh into large chunks.

Add the tomatoes and cream to the reserved liquid. Bring to the boil, then reduce the heat and simmer for 15 minutes, or until thickened.

Meanwhile, bring a large heavy-based saucepan of lightly salted water to the boil. Add the pasta, return to the boil and cook for 8–10 minutes, or until tender but still firm to the bite. Drain and transfer to a warmed serving dish.

Add the salmon and prawns to the tomato mixture and stir gently until coated in the sauce. Spoon the salmon sauce onto the pasta, toss lightly, then serve, garnished with dill sprigs.

SERVES 4

350 g/12 oz salmon fillet

fresh dill sprigs, plus extra to garnish

225 ml/8 fl oz dry white wine

6 tomatoes, peeled and chopped

150 ml/5 fl oz double cream

350 g/12 oz dried fusilli

115 g/4 oz cooked peeled prawns

salt and pepper

FETTUCCINE ALLA BUCANIERA

Spread the flour out on a plate and season with salt and pepper. Coat all the fish pieces with it, shaking off the excess. Melt the butter in a heavy-based saucepan or flameproof casserole. Add the fish, shallots, garlic, carrot and leek, then cook over a low heat, stirring frequently, for 10 minutes. Sprinkle in any remaining seasoned flour and cook, stirring constantly, for 1 minute.

Mix the stock, wine, anchovy essence and vinegar together in a jug and gradually stir into the fish mixture. Bring to the boil, stirring constantly, then reduce the heat and simmer gently for 15 minutes.

Meanwhile, bring a large heavy-based saucepan of lightly salted water to the boil. Add the pasta, return to the boil and cook for 8–10 minutes, or until tender but still firm to the bite. Drain and transfer to a warmed serving dish. Spoon the fish mixture onto the pasta, garnish with chopped parsley and serve immediately.

SERVES 6

1 tbsp plain flour

450 g/1 lb lemon sole fillets, skinned and cut into chunks

450 g/1 lb monkfish fillets, skinned and cut into chunks

85 g/3 oz unsalted butter

4 shallots, finely chopped

2 garlic cloves, crushed

1 carrot, diced

1 leek, finely chopped

300 ml/10 fl oz fish stock

300 ml/10 fl oz dry white wine

2 tsp anchovy essence

1 tbsp balsamic vinegar

450 g/1 lb dried fettuccine

salt and pepper

chopped fresh flat-leaf parsley, to garnish

FUSILLI WITH MONKFISH & BROCCOLI

SERVES 4

115 g/4 oz broccoli, divided into florets

3 tbsp olive oil

350 g/12 oz monkfish fillet, skinned and cut into bite-sized pieces

2 garlic cloves, crushed

125 ml/4 fl oz dry white wine

225 ml/8 fl oz double cream

400 g/14 oz dried fusilli

85 g/3 oz Gorgonzola cheese, diced

salt and pepper

Divide the broccoli florets into tiny sprigs. Bring a saucepan of lightly salted water to the boil, add the broccoli and cook for 2 minutes. Drain and refresh under cold running water.

Heat the oil in a large heavy-based frying pan. Add the monkfish and garlic and season to taste with salt and pepper. Cook, stirring frequently, for 5 minutes, or until the fish is opaque. Pour in the white wine and cream and cook, stirring occasionally, for 5 minutes, or until the fish is cooked through and the sauce has thickened. Stir in the broccoli florets.

Meanwhile, bring a large heavy-based saucepan of lightly salted water to the boil. Add the pasta, return to the boil and cook for 8–10 minutes, or until tender but still firm to the bite. Drain the pasta and tip into the saucepan with the fish, add the Gorgonzola cheese and toss lightly. Serve immediately.

SPRINGTIME PASTA

Fill a bowl with cold water and add the lemon juice. Prepare the artichokes one at a time. Cut off the stems and trim away any tough outer leaves. Cut across the tops of the leaves. Slice in half lengthways and remove the central fibrous chokes, then cut lengthways into 5 mm/¼ inch thick slices. Immediately place the slices in the bowl of acidulated water to prevent discoloration.

Heat 5 tablespoons of the oil in a heavy-based frying pan. Drain the artichoke slices and pat dry with kitchen paper. Add them to the frying pan with the shallots, garlic, parsley and mint and cook over a low heat, stirring frequently, for 10–12 minutes, until tender.

Meanwhile, bring a large saucepan of lightly salted water to the boil. Add the pasta, bring back to the boil and cook for 8–10 minutes, until tender but still firm to the bite.

Peel the prawns, cut a slit along the back of each and remove and discard the dark vein. Melt the butter in a small frying pan and add the prawns. Cook, stirring occasionally, for 2–3 minutes, until they have changed colour. Season to taste with salt and pepper.

Drain the pasta and tip it into a bowl. Add the remaining oil and toss well. Add the artichoke mixture and the prawns and toss again. Serve immediately.

SERVES 4

2 tbsp lemon juice

4 baby globe artichokes

7 tbsp olive oil

2 shallots, finely chopped

2 garlic cloves, finely chopped

2 tbsp chopped fresh flat-leaf parsley

2 tbsp chopped fresh mint

350 g/12 oz dried rigatoni

12 large raw prawns

25 g/1 oz unsalted butter

salt and pepper

TAGLIATELLE
IN A CREAMY PRAWN SAUCE

Heat the oil and butter in a saucepan over a medium–low heat. Add the garlic and red pepper. Cook for a few seconds until the garlic is just beginning to colour. Stir in the tomato purée and wine. Cook for 10 minutes, stirring.

Bring a large saucepan of lightly salted water to the boil. Add the pasta, bring back to the boil and cook for 8–10 minutes, or until tender but still firm to the bite. Drain and return to the pan.

Add the prawns to the sauce and increase the heat to medium–high. Cook for 2 minutes, stirring, until the prawns turn pink. Reduce the heat and stir in the cream. Cook for 1 minute, stirring constantly, until thickened. Season to taste with salt and pepper.

Transfer the pasta to a warmed serving dish. Pour the sauce over the pasta. Sprinkle with the parsley. Toss well to mix and serve immediately.

SERVES 4

3 tbsp olive oil

3 tbsp butter

4 garlic cloves, very finely chopped

2 tbsp finely diced red pepper

2 tbsp tomato purée

125 ml/4 fl oz dry white wine

450 g/1 lb dried tagliatelle

350 g/12 oz raw peeled prawns

125 ml/4 fl oz double cream

salt and pepper

3 tbsp chopped fresh flat-leaf parsley, to garnish

FETTUCCINE & PRAWN PARCELS

SERVES 4

450 g/1 lb dried fettuccine

150 ml/5 fl oz Pesto (see page 13)

4 tsp extra virgin olive oil

750 g/1 lb 10 oz large raw prawns, peeled and deveined

2 garlic cloves, crushed

125 ml/4 fl oz dry white wine

salt and pepper

Preheat the oven to 200°C/400°F/Gas Mark 6. Cut out four 30-cm/12-inch squares of greaseproof paper. Bring a large heavy-based saucepan of lightly salted water to the boil. Add the pasta, return to the boil and cook for 2–3 minutes, or until just softened. Drain and reserve until required.

Mix the fettuccine and half of the pesto together in a bowl. Spread out the paper squares and place 1 teaspoon of oil in the centre of each. Divide the fettuccine between the squares, then divide the prawns and place on top of the fettuccine. Mix the remaining pesto and the garlic together and spoon it over the prawns. Season each parcel to taste with salt and pepper and sprinkle with the white wine. Dampen the edges of the greaseproof paper and wrap the parcels loosely, twisting the edges to seal.

Place the parcels on a baking tray and bake in the preheated oven for 10–15 minutes. Transfer the parcels to plates and serve.

LINGUINE WITH PRAWNS & SCALLOPS

Peel and devein the prawns, reserving the shells. Melt the butter in a heavy-based frying pan. Add the shallots and cook over a low heat, stirring occasionally, for 5 minutes, or until softened. Add the prawn shells and cook, stirring constantly, for 1 minute. Pour in the vermouth and cook, stirring, for 1 minute. Add the water, bring to the boil, then reduce the heat and simmer for 10 minutes, or until the liquid has reduced by half. Remove the frying pan from the heat.

Bring a large heavy-based saucepan of lightly salted water to the boil. Add the pasta, return to the boil and cook for 8–10 minutes, or until tender but still firm to the bite.

Meanwhile, heat the oil in a separate heavy-based frying pan. Add the scallops and prawns and cook, stirring frequently, for 2 minutes, or until the scallops are opaque and the prawns have changed colour. Strain the prawn-shell stock into the frying pan. Drain the pasta and add to the frying pan with the chives and season to taste with salt and pepper. Toss well over a low heat for 1 minute, then serve.

SERVES 6

450 g/1 lb raw prawns

25 g/1 oz butter

2 shallots, finely chopped

225 ml/8 fl oz dry white vermouth

350 ml/12 fl oz water

450 g/1 lb dried linguine

2 tbsp olive oil

450 g/1 lb prepared scallops,
   thawed if frozen

2 tbsp snipped fresh chives

salt and pepper

FUSILLI WITH CAJUN SEAFOOD SAUCE

Heat the cream in a large saucepan over a medium heat, stirring constantly. When almost boiling, reduce the heat and add the spring onions, parsley, thyme, pepper, chilli flakes and salt. Simmer for 7–8 minutes, stirring, until thickened. Remove from the heat.

Bring a large saucepan of lightly salted water to the boil. Add the pasta, bring back to the boil and cook for 8–10 minutes, or until tender but still firm to the bite. Drain and return to the pan. Add the cream mixture and the cheeses to the pasta. Toss over a low heat until the cheeses have melted. Transfer to a warmed serving dish.

Heat the oil in a large frying pan over a medium–high heat. Add the prawns and scallops. Cook for 2–3 minutes, until the prawns have just turned pink.

Pour the seafood over the pasta and toss well to mix. Sprinkle with the basil. Serve immediately.

SERVES 4

500 ml/18 fl oz whipping cream

8 spring onions, thinly sliced

55 g/2 oz chopped fresh flat-leaf parsley

1 tbsp chopped fresh thyme

½ tbsp pepper

½–1 tsp dried chilli flakes

1 tsp salt

450 g/1 lb dried fusilli

40 g/1½ oz freshly grated Gruyère cheese

20 g/¾ oz freshly grated Parmesan cheese

2 tbsp olive oil

225 g/8 oz raw peeled prawns

225 g/8 oz scallops, sliced

1 tbsp shredded fresh basil, to garnish

LINGUINE WITH MIXED SEAFOOD

SERVES 4–6

2 tbsp olive oil

2 shallots, finely chopped

2 garlic cloves, finely chopped

1 small red chilli, deseeded and
finely chopped

200 g/7 oz canned chopped
tomatoes

½ bunch fresh flat-leaf parsley,
chopped, plus extra sprigs
to garnish

pinch of sugar

450 g/1 lb live mussels, scrubbed
and debearded

450 g/1 lb live clams, scrubbed

6 tbsp dry white wine

1 lemon, sliced

450 g/1 lb dried linguine

175 g/6 oz large cooked prawns,
shelled and deveined

salt and pepper

Heat the oil in a saucepan. Add the shallots, garlic and chilli and cook over a low heat, stirring occasionally, for 5 minutes. Increase the heat to medium, stir in the tomatoes, parsley and sugar and season to taste with salt and pepper. Bring to the boil, then cover and simmer, stirring occasionally, for 15–20 minutes.

Discard any mussels or clams with broken shells or any that refuse to close when tapped. Pour the wine into a large saucepan and add the lemon slices, mussels and clams. Cover and cook over a high heat, shaking the pan occasionally, for 5 minutes, until all the shellfish have opened. Using a slotted spoon, transfer the shellfish to a bowl and reserve the cooking liquid.

Discard any mussels and clams that remain closed. Reserve a few for the garnish and remove the remainder from their shells. Strain the cooking liquid through a muslin-lined sieve.

Bring a saucepan of lightly salted water to the boil. Add the pasta and cook for 8–10 minutes, until tender but still firm to the bite.

Meanwhile, stir the strained cooking liquid into the shallot and tomato mixture and bring to the boil, stirring constantly. Add the shelled mussels and clams and the prawns. Taste and adjust the seasoning, if necessary, and heat through gently.

Strain the pasta and return it to the pan. Add the shellfish mixture and toss well. Serve, garnished with the reserved shellfish and parsley sprigs.

PAPPARDELLE
WITH SCALLOPS
& PORCINI

Put the porcini and hot water in a bowl. Leave to soak for 20 minutes. Strain the mushrooms, reserving the soaking water, and chop roughly. Line a sieve with two pieces of kitchen paper and strain the mushroom water into a bowl.

Heat the oil and butter in a large frying pan over a medium heat. Add the scallops and cook for 2 minutes until just golden. Add the garlic and mushrooms, then cook for another minute.

Stir in the lemon juice, cream and 125 ml/4 fl oz of the mushroom water. Bring to the boil, then simmer over a medium heat for 2–3 minutes, stirring constantly, until the liquid is reduced by half. Season to taste with salt and pepper. Remove from the heat.

Bring a large saucepan of lightly salted water to the boil. Add the pasta, bring back to the boil and cook for 8–10 minutes, or until tender but still firm to the bite. Drain and transfer to a warmed serving dish. Briefly reheat the sauce and pour over the pasta. Sprinkle with the parsley and toss well to mix. Serve immediately.

SERVES 4

25 g/1 oz dried porcini mushrooms

500 ml/18 fl oz hot water

3 tbsp olive oil

3 tbsp butter

350 g/12 oz scallops, sliced

2 garlic cloves, very finely chopped

2 tbsp lemon juice

250 ml/9 fl oz double cream

350 g/12 oz dried pappardelle

salt and pepper

2 tbsp chopped fresh flat-leaf parsley, to serve

BAKED SCALLOPS WITH PASTA IN SHELLS

Preheat the oven to 180°C/350°F/Gas Mark 4. Remove the scallops from their shells. Scrape off the skirt and the black intestinal thread. Reserve the white part (the flesh) and the orange part (the coral or roe). Very carefully ease the flesh and coral from the shell with a short, but very strong, knife. Wash the shells thoroughly and dry them well. Put the shells on a baking tray, sprinkle lightly with 2 tablespoons of the oil and set aside.

Meanwhile, bring a large saucepan of lightly salted water to the boil. Add the pasta and remaining oil and cook for 8–10 minutes, or until tender but still firm to the bite. Drain and divide the cooked pasta between the scallop shells.

Put the scallops, stock and onion in an ovenproof dish and season to taste with pepper. Cover with foil and bake in the preheated oven for 8 minutes.

Remove the dish from the oven. Remove the foil, then use a slotted spoon to transfer the scallops to the shells. Add 1 tablespoon of the cooking liquid to each shell, then sprinkle over a little lemon juice, lemon rind and cream, and top with the Cheddar cheese.

Increase the oven temperature to 230°C/450°F/Gas Mark 8 and return the scallops to the oven for a further 4 minutes.

Serve the scallops in their shells with crusty brown bread.

SERVES 4

12 scallops

3 tbsp olive oil

350 g/12 oz dried conchiglie

150 ml/5 fl oz fish stock

1 onion, chopped

juice and finely grated rind of 2 lemons

150 ml/5 fl oz double cream

225 g/8 oz grated Cheddar cheese

salt and pepper

crusty brown bread, to serve

SPAGHETTI CON VONGOLE

SERVES 4

1 kg/2 lb 4 oz live clams, scrubbed

175 ml/6 fl oz water

175 ml/6 fl oz dry white wine

350 g/12 oz dried spaghetti

5 tbsp olive oil

2 garlic cloves, finely chopped

4 tbsp chopped fresh flat-leaf
    parsley

salt and pepper

Discard any clams with broken shells or any that refuse to close when tapped. Place the clams in a large heavy-based saucepan. Add the water and wine, then cover and cook over a high heat, shaking the saucepan occasionally, for 5 minutes, or until the shells have opened. Remove the clams with a slotted spoon and strain the liquid through a muslin-lined sieve into a small saucepan. Bring to the boil and cook until reduced by about half. Discard any clams that remain closed and remove the remainder from their shells.

Bring a large heavy-based saucepan of lightly salted water to the boil. Add the pasta, return to the boil and cook for 8–10 minutes, or until tender but still firm to the bite.

Meanwhile, heat the oil in a large heavy-based frying pan. Add the garlic and cook, stirring frequently, for 2 minutes. Add the parsley and the reduced cooking liquid and simmer gently. Drain the pasta and add it to the frying pan with the clams. Season to taste with salt and pepper and cook, stirring constantly, for 4 minutes, or until the pasta is coated and the clams have heated through. Transfer to a warmed serving dish and serve immediately.

LINGUINE
WITH CLAMS IN
TOMATO SAUCE

Discard any clams with broken shells or any that refuse to close when tapped. Pour the wine into a large heavy-based saucepan and add the garlic, half the parsley and the clams. Cover and cook over a high heat, shaking the saucepan occasionally, for 5 minutes, or until the shells have opened. Remove the clams with a slotted spoon, reserving the cooking liquid. Discard any that remain closed and remove half of the remainder from their shells. Keep the shelled and unshelled clams in separate covered bowls. Strain the cooking liquid through a muslin-lined sieve and reserve.

Heat the oil in a heavy-based saucepan. Add the onion and cook over a low heat for 5 minutes, or until softened. Add the tomatoes, chilli and reserved cooking liquid and season to taste with salt and pepper. Bring to the boil, partially cover the saucepan and simmer for 20 minutes.

Meanwhile, bring a large heavy-based saucepan of lightly salted water to the boil. Add the pasta, return to the boil and cook for 8–10 minutes, or until tender but still firm to the bite. Drain and transfer to a warmed serving dish.

Stir the shelled clams into the tomato sauce and heat through gently for 2–3 minutes. Pour over the pasta and toss. Garnish with the clams in their shells and remaining parsley. Serve.

SERVES 4

1 kg/2 lb 4 oz live clams, scrubbed

225 ml/8 fl oz dry white wine

2 garlic cloves, roughly chopped

4 tbsp chopped fresh flat-leaf parsley

2 tbsp olive oil

1 onion, chopped

8 plum tomatoes, peeled, deseeded and chopped

1 fresh red chilli, deseeded and chopped

350 g/12 oz dried linguine

salt and pepper

FETTUCCINE WITH SAFFRON MUSSELS

Place the saffron in a small bowl, add the hot water and leave to soak. Discard any mussels with broken shells or any that refuse to close when tapped, then place them in a large heavy-based saucepan. Add the cold water, cover and cook over a high heat, shaking the saucepan occasionally, for 5 minutes, or until the shells have opened. Remove the mussels with a slotted spoon, reserving the liquid. Discard any that remain closed and remove the remainder from their shells. Strain the cooking liquid through a muslin-lined sieve and reserve.

Heat the oil in a frying pan. Add the onion and cook over a low heat, stirring, for 5 minutes, or until softened. Sprinkle in the flour and cook, stirring, for 1 minute. Remove the pan from the heat. Mix the vermouth and saffron liquid together and gradually whisk into the flour mixture. Return to the heat and simmer, stirring, for 2–3 minutes, or until thickened. Stir in 4 tablespoons of the reserved cooking liquid, the Parmesan cheese, mussels and chives and season to taste with salt and pepper. Simmer for 4 minutes, or until heated through.

Meanwhile, bring a large saucepan of lightly salted water to the boil. Add the pasta, return to the boil and cook for 8–10 minutes, or until tender but still firm to the bite. Drain and transfer to a large warmed serving dish. Add the mussels and sauce, toss well, garnish with chives and serve immediately.

SERVES 4

pinch of saffron threads

175 ml/6 fl oz hot water

1 kg/2 lb 4 oz live mussels, scrubbed and debearded

125 ml/4 fl oz cold water

1 tbsp sunflower oil

1 small onion, finely chopped

2 tbsp plain flour

125 ml/4 fl oz dry white vermouth

4 tbsp freshly grated Parmesan cheese

2 tbsp snipped chives, plus extra to garnish

350 g/12 oz dried fettuccine

salt and pepper

CONCHIGLIE
WITH MUSSELS

SERVES 6

1.25 kg/2 lb 12 oz live mussels, scrubbed and debearded

225 ml/8 fl oz dry white wine

2 large onions, chopped

115 g/4 oz unsalted butter

6 large garlic cloves, finely chopped

5 tbsp chopped fresh parsley

300 ml/10 fl oz double cream

400 g/14 oz dried conchiglie

salt and pepper

Discard any mussels with broken shells or any that refuse to close when tapped. Place the mussels in a large heavy-based saucepan, together with the wine and half of the onions. Cover and cook over a medium heat, shaking the saucepan frequently, for 2–3 minutes, or until the shells open. Remove the saucepan from the heat. Drain the mussels and reserve the cooking liquid. Discard any mussels that remain closed. Strain the cooking liquid through a muslin-lined sieve into a bowl and reserve.

Melt the butter in a saucepan. Add the remaining onions and cook until translucent. Stir in the garlic and cook for 1 minute. Gradually stir in the reserved cooking liquid. Stir in the parsley and cream and season to taste with salt and pepper. Bring to simmering point over a low heat.

Meanwhile, bring a large saucepan of lightly salted water to the boil. Add the pasta and cook for 8–10 minutes, or until tender but still firm to the bite. Drain and keep warm.

Reserve a few mussels for the garnish and remove the remainder from their shells. Stir the shelled mussels into the cream sauce and warm briefly. Transfer the pasta to a serving dish. Pour over the sauce and toss to coat. Garnish with the reserved mussels and serve.

SPAGHETTI WITH CRAB

Using a sharp knife, scoop the meat from the crab shell into a bowl. Mix the white and brown meat together lightly and reserve.

Bring a large pan of lightly salted water to the boil over a medium heat. Add the pasta and cook for 8–10 minutes, or until tender but still firm to the bite. Drain thoroughly and return to the pan.

Meanwhile, heat 2 tablespoons of the oil in a frying pan over a low heat. Add the chilli and garlic and cook for 30 seconds, then add the crabmeat, parsley, lemon juice and lemon rind. Cook for 1 minute, until the crab is just heated through.

Add the crab mixture to the pasta with the remaining oil and season to taste with salt and pepper. Toss together thoroughly, transfer to a large warmed serving dish and garnish with lemon wedges. Serve immediately.

SERVES 4

1 dressed crab, about 450 g/
   1 lb including the shell

350 g/12 oz dried spaghetti

6 tbsp extra virgin olive oil

1 fresh red chilli, deseeded and
   finely chopped

2 garlic cloves, finely chopped

3 tbsp chopped fresh parsley

2 tbsp lemon juice

1 tsp finely grated lemon rind

salt and pepper

lemon wedges, to garnish

FARFALLINI BUTTERED LOBSTER

Preheat the oven to 160°C/325°F/Gas Mark 3. Discard the stomach sac, vein and gills from each lobster. Remove the meat from the tail and chop. Crack the claws and legs, remove the meat and chop. Transfer the meat to a bowl and add the lemon juice and lemon rind. Clean the shells and place in the oven to dry out.

Melt 25 g/1 oz of the butter in a frying pan. Add the breadcrumbs and cook for 3 minutes, until crisp and golden brown. Melt the remaining butter in a separate saucepan. Add the lobster meat and heat through gently. Add the brandy and cook for a further 3 minutes, then add the cream and season to taste with salt and pepper.

Meanwhile, bring a large saucepan of lightly salted water to the boil. Add the farfallini and cook for 8–10 minutes, or until tender but still firm to the bite. Drain and spoon the pasta into the clean lobster shells.

Preheat the grill to medium. Spoon the buttered lobster on top of the pasta and sprinkle with a little Parmesan cheese and the breadcrumbs. Grill for 2–3 minutes, or until golden brown. Transfer the lobster shells to a warmed serving dish, garnish with the lemon wedges and dill sprigs and serve immediately.

SERVES 4

2 lobsters (about 700 g/1 lb 9 oz each), split into halves

juice and grated rind of 1 lemon

115 g/4 oz butter

4 tbsp fresh white breadcrumbs

2 tbsp brandy

5 tbsp double cream or crème fraîche

450 g/1 lb dried farfallini

55 g/2 oz freshly grated Parmesan cheese

salt and pepper

lemon wedges and fresh dill sprigs, to garnish

PENNE WITH SQUID & TOMATOES

SERVES 4

225 g/8 oz dried penne

350 g/12 oz prepared squid

6 tbsp olive oil

2 onions, sliced

225 ml/8 fl oz fish or chicken
stock

150 ml/5 fl oz full-bodied red wine

400 g/14 oz canned chopped
tomatoes

2 tbsp tomato purée

1 tbsp chopped fresh marjoram

1 bay leaf

salt and pepper

2 tbsp chopped fresh parsley,
to garnish

Bring a large heavy-based saucepan of lightly salted water to the boil. Add the pasta, return to the boil and cook for 3 minutes, then drain and reserve until required. With a sharp knife, cut the squid into strips.

Heat the oil in a large saucepan. Add the onions and cook over a low heat, stirring occasionally, for 5 minutes, or until softened. Add the squid and stock, bring to the boil and simmer for 3 minutes. Stir in the wine, tomatoes and their can juices, tomato purée, marjoram and bay leaf. Season to taste with salt and pepper. Bring to the boil and cook for 5 minutes, or until slightly reduced.

Add the pasta, return to the boil and simmer for 5–7 minutes, or until tender but still firm to the bite. Remove and discard the bay leaf. Transfer to a warmed serving dish, garnish with the parsley and serve immediately.

VEGETARIAN

SPAGHETTI OLIO E AGLIO

Bring a large heavy-based saucepan of lightly salted water to the boil. Add the pasta, return to the boil and cook for 8–10 minutes, or until tender but still firm to the bite.

Meanwhile, heat the oil in a heavy-based frying pan. Add the garlic and a pinch of salt and cook over a low heat, stirring constantly, for 3–4 minutes, or until golden. Do not allow the garlic to brown or it will taste bitter. Remove the frying pan from the heat.

Drain the pasta and transfer to a warmed serving dish. Pour in the garlic-flavoured oil, then add the chopped parsley and season to taste with salt and pepper. Toss well and serve immediately.

SERVES 4

450 g/1 lb dried spaghetti

125 ml/4 fl oz extra virgin olive oil

3 garlic cloves, finely chopped

3 tbsp chopped fresh flat-leaf parsley

salt and pepper

FETTUCCINE ALL' ALFREDO

Put the butter and 150 ml/5 fl oz of the cream into a large pan and bring the mixture to the boil over a medium heat. Reduce the heat, then simmer gently for 1½ minutes, or until the cream has thickened slightly.

Meanwhile, bring a large pan of lightly salted water to the boil over a medium heat. Add the pasta and cook for 8–10 minutes, or until tender but still firm to the bite. Drain thoroughly and return to the pan, then pour over the cream sauce.

Toss the pasta in the sauce over a low heat, stirring with a wooden spoon, until coated thoroughly.

Add the remaining cream, Parmesan cheese and nutmeg to the pasta mixture and season to taste with salt and pepper. Toss the pasta in the mixture while heating through.

Transfer the pasta mixture to a warmed serving plate and garnish with the fresh parsley sprig. Serve immediately with extra grated Parmesan cheese.

SERVES 4

2 tbsp butter

200 ml/7 fl oz double cream

450 g/1 lb dried fettuccine

85 g/3 oz freshly grated Parmesan cheese, plus extra to serve

pinch of freshly grated nutmeg

salt and pepper

1 fresh flat-leaf parsley sprig, to garnish

CREAMY PAPPARDELLE WITH BROCCOLI

SERVES 4

55 g/2 oz butter

1 large onion, finely chopped

450 g/1 lb dried pappardelle

450 g/1 lb broccoli, broken into florets

150 ml/5 fl oz vegetable stock

1 tbsp plain flour

150 ml/5 fl oz single cream

55 g/2 oz freshly grated mozzarella cheese

freshly grated nutmeg

salt and white pepper

fresh apple slices, to garnish

Melt half the butter in a large pan over a medium heat. Add the onion and cook for 4 minutes.

Add the pasta and broccoli to the pan and cook, stirring constantly, for 2 minutes. Add the stock, bring back to the boil and simmer for 8–10 minutes. Season well with salt and white pepper.

Meanwhile, melt the remaining butter in a pan over a medium heat. Sprinkle over the flour and cook, stirring constantly, for 2 minutes. Gradually stir in the cream and bring to simmering point, but do not boil. Add the mozzarella cheese and season to taste with salt, white pepper and a little freshly grated nutmeg.

Drain the pasta and broccoli mixture and return to the pan. Pour over the cheese sauce. Cook, stirring occasionally, for 2 minutes. Transfer the pasta and broccoli mixture to a large warmed serving dish and garnish with a few slices of apple. Serve immediately.

RIGATONI WITH GORGONZOLA SAUCE

Bring a large heavy-based saucepan of lightly salted water to the boil. Add the pasta, return to the boil and cook for 8–10 minutes, until tender but still firm to the bite.

Meanwhile, melt the butter in a separate heavy-based saucepan. Add the sage leaves and cook, stirring gently, for 1 minute. Remove and reserve the sage leaves. Add the cheese and cook, stirring constantly, over a low heat until it has melted. Gradually, stir in 175 ml/6 fl oz of the cream and the vermouth. Season to taste with salt and pepper and cook, stirring, until thickened. Add more cream if the sauce seems too thick.

Drain the pasta well and transfer to a warmed serving dish. Add the Gorgonzola sauce, toss well to mix and serve immediately, garnished with the reserved sage leaves.

SERVES 4

400 g/14 oz dried rigatoni

25 g/1 oz unsalted butter

6 fresh sage leaves

200 g/7 oz Gorgonzola cheese, diced

175–225 ml/6–8 fl oz double cream

2 tbsp dry vermouth

salt and pepper

PENNE WITH ASPARAGUS & GORGONZOLA

Preheat the oven to 230°C/450°F/Gas Mark 8. Place the asparagus tips in a single layer in a shallow ovenproof dish. Sprinkle with the oil and season to taste with salt and pepper. Turn to coat in the oil and seasoning. Roast in the preheated oven for 10–12 minutes until slightly browned and just tender. Set aside and keep warm.

Combine the crumbled cheese with the cream in a bowl. Season to taste with salt and pepper.

Bring a large saucepan of lightly salted water to a boil. Add the pasta, bring back to a boil and cook for 8–10 minutes, or until tender but still firm to the bite. Drain and transfer to a warmed serving dish. Immediately add the asparagus and the cheese mixture. Toss well until the cheese has melted and the pasta is coated with the sauce. Serve immediately.

SERVES 4

450 g/1 lb asparagus tips

1 tbsp olive oil

225 g/8 oz Gorgonzola cheese, crumbled

175 ml/6 fl oz double cream

350 g/12 oz dried penne

salt and pepper

SPAGHETTI WITH RICOTTA

SERVES 4

350 g/12 oz dried spaghetti

40 g/1½ oz butter

2 tbsp chopped fresh flat-leaf parsley, plus extra sprigs to garnish

125 g/4½ oz freshly ground almonds

125 g/4½ oz ricotta cheese

pinch of grated nutmeg

pinch of ground cinnamon

150 ml/5 fl oz crème fraîche

3 tbsp olive oil

125 ml/4 fl oz vegetable stock

1 tbsp pine kernels

salt and pepper

Bring a large heavy-based saucepan of lightly salted water to the boil. Add the spaghetti, return to the boil and cook for 8–10 minutes, or until tender but still firm to the bite.

Drain the pasta, return to the saucepan and toss with the butter and chopped parsley. Keep warm.

To make the sauce, mix the ground almonds, ricotta cheese, nutmeg, cinnamon and crème fraîche together in a small saucepan over a low heat to form a thick paste. Gradually stir in the oil. When the oil has been fully incorporated, gradually stir in the stock, until the sauce is smooth. Season to taste with pepper.

Transfer the spaghetti to a warmed serving dish, pour over the sauce and toss together well. Sprinkle over the pine kernels, garnish with the parsley sprigs and serve warm.

RIGATONI WITH PEPPERS & GOAT'S CHEESE

Heat the oil and butter in a large frying pan over a medium heat. Add the onion and cook until soft. Increase the heat to medium–high and add the peppers and garlic. Cook for 12–15 minutes, stirring, until the peppers are tender but not mushy. Season to taste with salt and pepper. Remove from the heat.

Bring a large saucepan of lightly salted water to the boil. Add the pasta, bring back to the boil and cook for 8–10 minutes, or until tender but still firm to the bite. Drain and transfer to a warmed serving dish. Add the goat's cheese and toss to mix.

Briefly reheat the sauce. Add the basil and olives. Pour over the pasta and toss well to mix. Serve immediately.

SERVES 4

2 tbsp olive oil

1 tbsp butter

1 small onion, finely chopped

4 peppers, yellow and red, deseeded and cut into 2-cm/ ¾-inch squares

3 garlic cloves, thinly sliced

450 g/1 lb dried rigatoni

125 g/4½ oz goat's cheese, crumbled

15 fresh basil leaves, shredded

10 black olives, stoned and sliced

salt and pepper

LINGUINE WITH WILD MUSHROOMS

VEGETARIAN

Melt the butter in a large heavy-based frying pan. Add the onion and garlic and cook over a low heat for 5 minutes, or until softened. Add the mushrooms and cook, stirring occasionally, for a further 10 minutes.

Meanwhile, bring a large heavy-based saucepan of lightly salted water to the boil. Add the pasta, return to the boil and cook for 8–10 minutes, or until tender but still firm to the bite.

Stir the crème fraîche, basil and Parmesan cheese into the mushroom mixture and season to taste with salt and pepper. Cover and heat through gently for 1–2 minutes. Drain the pasta and transfer to a warmed serving dish. Add the mushroom mixture and toss lightly. Garnish with extra basil and serve immediately with extra Parmesan cheese.

SERVES 4

55 g/2 oz butter

1 onion, chopped

1 garlic clove, finely chopped

350 g/12 oz wild mushrooms, sliced

350 g/12 oz dried linguine

300 ml/10 fl oz crème fraîche

2 tbsp shredded fresh basil leaves, plus extra to garnish

4 tbsp freshly grated Parmesan cheese, plus extra to serve

salt and pepper

PENNE WITH CREAMY MUSHROOMS

SERVES 4

55 g/2 oz butter

1 tbsp olive oil

6 shallots, sliced

450 g/1 lb chestnut mushrooms, sliced

1 tsp plain flour

150 ml/5 fl oz double cream

2 tbsp port

115 g/4 oz sun-dried tomatoes in oil, drained and chopped

pinch of freshly grated nutmeg

350 g/12 oz dried penne

salt and pepper

2 tbsp chopped fresh flat-leaf parsley, to garnish

Melt the butter with the oil in a large heavy-based frying pan. Add the shallots and cook over a low heat, stirring occasionally, for 4–5 minutes, or until softened. Add the mushrooms and cook over a low heat for a further 2 minutes. Season to taste with salt and pepper, sprinkle in the flour and cook, stirring, for 1 minute.

Remove the frying pan from the heat and gradually stir in the cream and port. Return to the heat, add the sun-dried tomatoes and grated nutmeg and cook over a low heat, stirring occasionally, for 8 minutes.

Meanwhile, bring a large heavy-based saucepan of lightly salted water to the boil. Add the pasta, return to the boil and cook for 8–10 minutes, or until tender but still firm to the bite. Drain the pasta well and add to the mushroom sauce. Cook for 3 minutes, then transfer to a warmed serving dish. Sprinkle with the chopped parsley and serve immediately.

TAGLIATELLE WITH WALNUT SAUCE

Place the breadcrumbs, walnuts, garlic, milk, oil and fromage frais in a large mortar and grind to a smooth paste with a pestle. Alternatively, place the ingredients in a food processor and process until smooth. Stir in the cream to give a thick sauce consistency and season to taste with salt and pepper. Reserve.

Bring a large heavy-based saucepan of lightly salted water to the boil. Add the pasta, return to the boil and cook for 8–10 minutes, or until tender but still firm to the bite.

Drain the pasta and transfer to a warmed serving dish. Add the walnut sauce and toss thoroughly to coat. Serve immediately.

SERVES 4

25 g/1 oz fresh white breadcrumbs

350 g/12 oz walnut pieces

2 garlic cloves, finely chopped

4 tbsp milk

4 tbsp olive oil

85 g/3 oz fromage frais or cream cheese

150 ml/5 fl oz single cream

350 g/12 oz dried tagliatelle

salt and pepper

TAGLIATELLE
WITH GARLIC
CRUMBS

Mix the breadcrumbs, parsley, chives and marjoram together in
a small bowl.

Heat the oil in a large heavy-based frying pan. Add the
breadcrumb mixture and the garlic and pine kernels, season to
taste with salt and pepper and cook over a low heat, stirring
constantly, for 5 minutes, or until the breadcrumbs become
golden, but not crisp. Remove the frying pan from the heat and
cover to keep warm.

Bring a large heavy-based saucepan of lightly salted water
to the boil. Add the pasta, return to the boil and cook for
8–10 minutes, or until tender but still firm to the bite.

Drain the pasta and transfer to a warmed serving dish. Drizzle
with a little oil and toss to mix. Add the garlic breadcrumbs and
toss again. Serve immediately with the grated pecorino cheese.

SERVES 4

350 g/12 oz fresh white
   breadcrumbs

4 tbsp finely chopped fresh
   flat-leaf parsley

1 tbsp snipped fresh chives

2 tbsp finely chopped fresh
   marjoram

3 tbsp olive oil, plus extra to serve

3–4 garlic cloves, finely chopped

55 g/2 oz pine kernels

450 g/1 lb dried tagliatelle,
   preferably a mixture of green
   and white

salt and pepper

55 g/2 oz freshly grated pecorino
   cheese, to serve

SPAGHETTI WITH ROCKET & HAZELNUT PESTO

SERVES 4

2 garlic cloves

85 g/3 oz hazelnuts

150 g/5 oz rocket, coarse stalks removed

115 g/4 oz freshly grated Parmesan cheese, plus extra to serve

6 tbsp extra virgin olive oil

115 g/4 oz mascarpone cheese

400 g/14 oz dried spaghetti

salt and pepper

Put the garlic and hazelnuts in a food processor and process until finely chopped. Add the rocket, Parmesan cheese and oil and process until smooth and thoroughly combined. Scrape the pesto into a serving dish, season to taste with salt and pepper and stir in the mascarpone cheese.

Bring a large saucepan of lightly salted water to the boil. Add the pasta, bring back to the boil and cook for 8–10 minutes, until tender but still firm to the bite.

Stir 100–150 ml/3½–5 fl oz of the pasta cooking water into the pesto, mixing well until thoroughly combined. Drain the pasta, add to the bowl and toss well to coat. Sprinkle with more Parmesan cheese and serve immediately.

SPAGHETTINI WITH CHILLI, TOMATOES & BLACK OLIVES

VEGETARIAN

204

Heat the oil in a large heavy-based frying pan. Add the garlic and cook over a low heat for 30 seconds, then add the capers, olives, dried chilli and tomatoes and season to taste with salt. Partially cover the pan and simmer gently for 20 minutes.

Stir in the parsley, partially cover the frying pan again and simmer for a further 10 minutes.

Meanwhile, bring a large heavy-based saucepan of lightly salted water to the boil. Add the pasta, return to the boil and cook for 5 minutes, or until tender but still firm to the bite. Drain and transfer to a warmed serving dish. Add the tomato and olive sauce and toss well. Sprinkle the Parmesan cheese over the pasta and garnish with extra chopped parsley. Serve immediately.

SERVES 4

1 tbsp olive oil

1 garlic clove, finely chopped

2 tsp bottled capers, drained, rinsed and chopped

12 black olives, stoned and chopped

½ dried red chilli, crushed

1.25 kg/2 lb 12 oz canned chopped tomatoes

1 tbsp chopped fresh parsley, plus extra to garnish

350 g/12 oz dried spaghettini

2 tbsp freshly grated Parmesan cheese

salt

NEAPOLITAN
CONCHIGLIE

Place the tomatoes in a large heavy-based saucepan. Add the wine, onion, carrot, celery, parsley and sugar and gradually bring to the boil, stirring frequently. Reduce the heat, partially cover and simmer, stirring occasionally, for 45 minutes, or until thickened.

Meanwhile, bring a large heavy-based saucepan of lightly salted water to the boil. Add the pasta, return to the boil and cook for 8–10 minutes, or until tender but still firm to the bite.

Rub the tomato sauce through a sieve with the back of a wooden spoon into a clean saucepan and stir in the marjoram. Reheat gently, stirring occasionally, for 1–2 minutes. Drain the pasta and transfer to a warmed serving dish. Pour the tomato sauce over the pasta and toss well. Sprinkle with Parmesan cheese and serve immediately.

SERVES 4

900 g/2 lb plum tomatoes, roughly chopped

150 ml/5 fl oz dry white wine

1 onion, chopped

1 carrot, chopped

1 celery stick, chopped

2 fresh flat-leaf parsley sprigs

pinch of sugar

350 g/12 oz dried conchiglie

1 tbsp chopped fresh marjoram

salt

freshly grated Parmesan cheese, to serve

SPAGHETTI
WITH TOMATO &
BASIL SAUCE

SERVES 4

5 tbsp extra virgin olive oil

1 onion, finely chopped

800 g/1 lb 12 oz canned chopped
tomatoes

4 garlic cloves, cut into quarters

450 g/1 lb dried spaghetti

large handful fresh basil leaves,
shredded

salt and pepper

freshly grated Parmesan cheese,
to serve

Heat the oil in a large saucepan over a medium heat. Add the
onion and cook gently for 5 minutes, until soft. Add the tomatoes
and garlic. Bring to the boil, then simmer over a medium–low
heat for 25–30 minutes, or until the oil separates from the
tomatoes. Season to taste with salt and pepper.

Bring a large saucepan of lightly salted water to the boil. Add
the pasta, bring back to the boil and cook for 8–10 minutes,
or until tender but still firm to the bite. Drain and transfer to a
warmed serving dish.

Pour the sauce over the pasta. Add the basil and toss well to
mix. Serve with the Parmesan cheese.

FUSILLI WITH SUN-DRIED TOMATOES

Put the sun-dried tomatoes in a bowl, pour over the boiling water and leave to stand for 5 minutes. Using a slotted spoon, remove one third of the tomatoes from the bowl. Cut into bite-sized pieces. Put the remaining tomatoes and water into a blender and purée.

Heat the oil in a large frying pan over a medium heat. Add the onion and cook gently for 5 minutes, or until soft. Add the garlic and cook until just beginning to colour. Add the puréed tomato and the reserved tomato pieces to the pan. Bring to the boil, then simmer over a medium–low heat for 10 minutes. Stir in the herbs and season to taste with salt and pepper. Simmer for 1 minute, then remove from the heat.

Bring a large saucepan of lightly salted water to the boil. Add the pasta, bring back to the boil and cook for 8–10 minutes, or until tender but still firm to the bite. Drain and transfer to a warmed serving dish. Briefly reheat the sauce. Pour over the pasta, add the basil and toss well to mix. Sprinkle with the Parmesan cheese and serve immediately.

SERVES 4

85 g/3 oz sun-dried tomatoes (not in oil)

700 ml/1¼ pints boiling water

2 tbsp olive oil

1 onion, finely chopped

2 large garlic cloves, finely sliced

2 tbsp chopped fresh flat-leaf parsley

2 tsp chopped fresh oregano

1 tsp chopped fresh rosemary

350 g/12 oz dried fusilli

10 fresh basil leaves, shredded

salt and pepper

freshly grated Parmesan cheese, to serve

LINGUINE WITH GARLIC & RED PEPPERS

Preheat the oven to 200°C/400°F/Gas Mark 6. Place the unpeeled garlic cloves in a shallow ovenproof dish. Roast in the preheated oven for 7–10 minutes, or until the garlic cloves feel soft.

Put the peppers, tomatoes and oil in a food processor or blender, then purée. Squeeze the garlic flesh into the purée. Add the chilli flakes and thyme. Season to taste with salt and pepper. Blend again, then scrape into a saucepan and set aside.

Bring a large saucepan of lightly salted water to the boil. Add the pasta, bring back to the boil and cook for 8–10 minutes, or until tender but still firm to the bite. Drain and transfer to a warmed serving dish.

Reheat the sauce and pour over the pasta. Toss well to mix and serve immediately.

SERVES 4

6 large garlic cloves, unpeeled

400 g/14 oz bottled roasted red peppers, drained and sliced

200 g/7 oz canned chopped tomatoes

3 tbsp olive oil

¼ tsp dried chilli flakes

1 tsp chopped fresh thyme or oregano

350 g/12 oz dried linguine

salt and pepper

FETTUCCINE WITH OLIVES & PEPPERS

SERVES 4

100 ml/3½ fl oz olive oil

1 onion, finely chopped

200 g/7 oz black olives, stoned
and roughly chopped

400 g/14 oz canned chopped
tomatoes, drained

2 red, yellow or orange peppers,
deseeded and cut into thin
strips

350 g/12 oz dried fettuccine

salt and pepper

freshly grated pecorino cheese,
to serve

Heat the oil in a large heavy-based saucepan. Add the onion and
cook over a low heat, stirring occasionally, for 5 minutes, or until
softened. Add the olives, tomatoes and peppers and season to
taste with salt and pepper. Cover and simmer gently over a very
low heat, stirring occasionally, for 35 minutes.

Meanwhile, bring a large heavy-based saucepan of lightly
salted water to the boil. Add the pasta, return to the boil and
cook for 8–10 minutes, or until tender but still firm to the bite.
Drain the pasta and transfer to a warmed serving dish.

Spoon the sauce onto the pasta and toss well. Serve
immediately with the grated pecorino cheese.

OLIVE, PEPPER & CHERRY TOMATO PASTA

Bring a large heavy-based saucepan of lightly salted water to the boil. Add the pasta, return to the boil and cook for 8–10 minutes, or until tender but still firm to the bite. Drain the pasta thoroughly.

Heat the oil and butter in a frying pan until the butter melts. Sauté the garlic for 30 seconds. Add the peppers and cook, stirring constantly, for 3–4 minutes.

Stir in the cherry tomatoes, oregano, wine and olives and cook for 3–4 minutes. Season well with salt and pepper and stir in the rocket until just wilted. Transfer the pasta to a serving dish, spoon over the sauce and garnish with oregano sprigs. Serve.

SERVES 4

225 g/8 oz dried penne

2 tbsp olive oil

25 g/1 oz butter

2 garlic cloves, crushed

1 green pepper, deseeded and thinly sliced

1 yellow pepper, deseeded and thinly sliced

16 cherry tomatoes, halved

1 tbsp chopped fresh oregano, plus extra sprigs to garnish

125 ml/4 fl oz dry white wine

2 tbsp quartered, stoned black olives

75 g/2¾ oz rocket

salt and pepper

ARTICHOKE
& OLIVE
SPAGHETTI

Heat 1 tablespoon of the oil in a large frying pan and gently cook the onion, garlic, lemon juice and aubergines for 4–5 minutes, or until lightly browned.

Pour in the passata, season to taste with salt and pepper and add the sugar and tomato purée. Bring to the boil, reduce the heat and simmer for 20 minutes. Gently stir in the artichoke halves and olives and cook for 5 minutes.

Meanwhile, bring a large heavy-based saucepan of lightly salted water to the boil. Add the spaghetti, return to the boil and cook for 8–10 minutes, or until just tender but still firm to the bite. Drain well, toss in the remaining oil and season to taste with salt and pepper. Transfer the spaghetti to a warmed serving bowl and top with the vegetable sauce. Garnish with basil sprigs and serve with olive bread.

SERVES 4

2 tbsp olive oil

1 large red onion, chopped

2 garlic cloves, crushed

1 tbsp lemon juice

4 baby aubergines, quartered

600 ml/1 pint passata

2 tsp caster sugar

2 tbsp tomato purée

400 g/14 oz canned artichoke
  hearts, drained and halved

125 g/4½ oz stoned black olives

350 g/12 oz dried wholemeal
  spaghetti

salt and pepper

fresh basil sprigs, to garnish

olive bread, to serve

SPAGHETTI ALLA NORMA

SERVES 4

175 ml/6 fl oz olive oil

500 g/1 lb 2 oz plum tomatoes,
  peeled and chopped

1 garlic clove, chopped

350 g/12 oz aubergines, diced

400 g/14 oz dried spaghetti

½ bunch fresh basil, torn

115 g/4 oz freshly grated pecorino
  cheese

salt and pepper

Heat 4 tablespoons of the oil in a large saucepan. Add the
tomatoes and garlic, season to taste with salt and pepper, cover
and cook over a low heat, stirring occasionally, for 25 minutes.

Meanwhile, heat the remaining oil in a heavy-based frying pan.
Add the aubergines and cook, stirring occasionally, for 5 minutes,
until evenly golden brown. Remove with a slotted spoon and
drain on kitchen paper.

Bring a large pan of salted water to the boil. Add the pasta,
bring back to the boil and cook for 8–10 minutes, until tender but
still firm to the bite.

Meanwhile, stir the drained aubergines into the tomato
mixture. Taste and adjust the seasoning, if necessary.

Drain the pasta and place in a warmed serving dish. Add
the tomato and aubergine mixture, basil and half the pecorino
cheese. Toss well, sprinkle with the remaining cheese and
serve immediately.

LINGUINE & MARINATED AUBERGINE

Place the stock, wine vinegar and balsamic vinegar in a large heavy-based saucepan and bring to the boil over a low heat. Add 2 teaspoons of the olive oil and the oregano sprig and simmer gently for 1 minute. Add the aubergine slices to the saucepan, remove from the heat and leave to stand for 10 minutes.

Meanwhile make the marinade. Mix the extra virgin olive oil, garlic, chopped oregano, almonds, red pepper, lime juice, orange rind and orange juice together in a large bowl and season to taste with salt and pepper.

Carefully remove the aubergine from the saucepan with a slotted spoon and drain well. Add the aubergine slices to the marinade, mixing well, and leave to marinate in the refrigerator for 12 hours.

Bring a large heavy-based saucepan of lightly salted water to the boil. Add half of the remaining olive oil and the linguine, return to the boil and cook for 8–10 minutes, or until just tender but still firm to the bite.

Drain the pasta thoroughly and toss with the remaining olive oil while still warm. Arrange the pasta on a serving plate with the aubergine slices and the marinade and serve.

SERVES 4

150 ml/5 fl oz vegetable stock

150 ml/5 fl oz white wine vinegar

2 tsp balsamic vinegar

3 tbsp olive oil

1 fresh oregano sprig

450 g/1 lb aubergine, peeled and thinly sliced

400 g/14 oz dried linguine

salt

marinade

2 tbsp extra virgin olive oil

2 garlic cloves, crushed

2 tbsp chopped fresh oregano

2 tbsp finely chopped roasted almonds

2 tbsp diced red pepper

2 tbsp lime juice

grated rind and juice of 1 orange

salt and pepper

FARFALLE WITH AUBERGINES

Place the aubergine in a colander, sprinkling each layer with salt, and leave to drain for 30 minutes. Meanwhile, heat 1 tablespoon of the oil in a heavy-based saucepan. Add the shallots and garlic and cook over a low heat, stirring occasionally, for 5 minutes, or until softened. Add the tomatoes and their can juices, stir in the sugar and season to taste with salt and pepper. Cover and simmer gently, stirring occasionally, for 30 minutes, or until thickened.

Rinse the aubergine under cold running water, drain well and pat dry with kitchen paper. Heat half the remaining oil in a heavy-based frying pan, then add the aubergine in batches, and cook, stirring frequently, until golden brown all over. Remove from the frying pan with a slotted spoon and keep warm while you cook the remaining batches, adding the remaining oil as necessary.

Meanwhile, bring a large heavy-based saucepan of lightly salted water to the boil. Add the pasta, return to the boil and cook for 8–10 minutes, or until tender but still firm to the bite. Drain the pasta and transfer to a warmed serving dish.

Pour the tomato sauce over the pasta and toss well to mix. Top with the diced aubergine, garnish with fresh basil sprigs and serve.

SERVES 4

1 large or 2 medium aubergines, diced

150 ml/5 fl oz olive oil

4 shallots, chopped

2 garlic cloves, finely chopped

400 g/14 oz canned chopped tomatoes

1 tsp caster sugar

350 g/12 oz dried farfalle

salt and pepper

fresh basil sprigs, to garnish

FUSILLI WITH COURGETTE & LEMON

SERVES 4

6 tbsp olive oil

1 small onion, very thinly sliced

2 garlic cloves, very finely
    chopped

2 tbsp chopped fresh rosemary

1 tbsp chopped fresh flat-leaf
    parsley

450 g/1 lb small courgettes,
    cut into strips measuring
    4 cm x 5 mm/1½ x ¼ inches

finely grated rind of 1 lemon

450 g/1 lb dried fusilli

salt and pepper

4 tbsp freshly grated Parmesan
    cheese, to serve

Heat the oil in a large frying pan over a medium–low heat. Add the onion and cook gently, stirring occasionally, for about 10 minutes, until golden.

Increase the heat to medium–high. Add the garlic, rosemary and parsley. Cook for a few seconds, stirring.

Add the courgettes and lemon rind. Cook for 5–7 minutes, stirring occasionally, until the courgettes are just tender. Season to taste with salt and pepper. Remove from the heat.

Bring a large saucepan of lightly salted water to the boil. Add the pasta, bring back to the boil and cook for 8–10 minutes, or until tender but still firm to the bite. Drain and transfer to a warmed serving dish.

Briefly reheat the courgette sauce. Pour over the pasta and toss well to mix. Sprinkle with the Parmesan cheese and serve immediately.

TAGLIATELLE WITH COURGETTES & TOMATOES

Heat the oil in a large heavy-based frying pan. Add the onion and garlic and cook over a low heat, stirring occasionally, for 5 minutes, or until softened. Add the courgettes and cook, stirring, for a further 3 minutes.

Add the tomatoes and season to taste with salt and cayenne pepper. Stir in the basil, cover and cook for 10–15 minutes, or until all the vegetables are tender.

Meanwhile, bring a large heavy-based saucepan of lightly salted water to the boil. Add the pasta, return to the boil and cook for 8–10 minutes, or until tender but still firm to the bite. Drain the pasta and transfer to a warmed serving dish. Add the courgette and tomato sauce and toss well. Sprinkle with the Parmesan cheese and serve immediately.

SERVES 4

4 tbsp olive oil

1 red onion, chopped

1 garlic clove, finely chopped

500 g/1 lb 2 oz courgettes, diced

2 beef tomatoes, peeled, deseeded and finely chopped

pinch of cayenne pepper

1 tbsp shredded fresh basil leaves

350 g/12 oz dried tagliatelle

salt

85 g/3 oz freshly grated Parmesan cheese, to serve

VERMICELLI
WITH
VEGETABLE
RIBBONS

Bring a large heavy-based saucepan of lightly salted water to the boil. Add the pasta, return to the boil and cook for 5 minutes, or until tender but still firm to the bite.

Meanwhile, cut the courgettes and carrots into very thin strips with a swivel-blade vegetable peeler or a mandolin. Melt the butter with the oil in a heavy-based frying pan. Add the carrot strips and garlic and cook over a low heat, stirring occasionally, for 5 minutes. Add the courgette strips and all the herbs and season to taste with salt and pepper.

Drain the pasta and add it to the frying pan. Toss well to mix and cook, stirring occasionally, for 5 minutes. Transfer to a warmed serving dish, add the radicchio, toss well and serve immediately.

SERVES 4

350 g/12 oz dried vermicelli

3 courgettes

3 carrots

25 g/1 oz unsalted butter

1 tbsp olive oil

2 garlic cloves, finely chopped

85 g/3 oz fresh basil, shredded

25 g/1 oz fresh chives, finely snipped

25 g/1 oz fresh flat-leaf parsley, finely chopped

1 small head radicchio, leaves shredded

salt and pepper

PASTA WITH GREEN VEGETABLES

SERVES 4

225 g/8 oz dried fusilli

1 head broccoli, cut into florets

2 courgettes, sliced

225 g/8 oz asparagus spears, trimmed

125 g/4½ oz mangetout

125 g/4½ oz frozen peas

25 g/1 oz butter

3 tbsp vegetable stock

5 tbsp double cream

large pinch of freshly grated nutmeg

2 tbsp chopped fresh parsley

salt and pepper

2 tbsp freshly grated Parmesan cheese, to serve

Bring a large heavy-based saucepan of lightly salted water to the boil. Add the pasta, return to the boil and cook for 8–10 minutes, or until tender but still firm to the bite. Drain the pasta in a colander, return to the saucepan, cover and keep warm.

Steam the broccoli, courgettes, asparagus spears and mangetout over a saucepan of boiling, salted water until just beginning to soften. Remove from the heat and plunge into cold water to prevent further cooking. Drain and reserve. Cook the peas in boiling, salted water for 3 minutes, then drain. Refresh in cold water and drain again.

Place the butter and stock in a saucepan over a medium heat. Add all the vegetables except for the asparagus spears and toss carefully with a wooden spoon to heat through, taking care not to break them up. Stir in the cream, allow the sauce to heat through and season to taste with salt, pepper and nutmeg.

Transfer the pasta to a warmed serving dish and stir in the chopped parsley. Spoon the sauce over and arrange the asparagus spears on top. Sprinkle with the freshly grated Parmesan cheese and serve hot.

SAFFRON TAGLIATELLE WITH ASPARAGUS

Place the saffron in a small bowl, stir in the hot water and leave to soak. Trim off and reserve 5 cm/2 inches of the asparagus tips and slice the remainder.

Melt the butter in a heavy-based saucepan. Add the onion and cook over a low heat, stirring occasionally, for 5 minutes, or until softened. Add the wine, cream and saffron mixture. Bring to the boil, stirring constantly, then reduce the heat and simmer for 5 minutes, or until slightly thickened. Stir in the lemon rind and juice and season to taste with salt and pepper.

Meanwhile, bring a large heavy-based saucepan of lightly salted water to the boil. Add the reserved asparagus tips and cook for 1 minute. Remove with a slotted spoon and add to the cream sauce. Cook the peas and sliced asparagus in the boiling water for 8 minutes, or until tender. With a slotted spoon, transfer them to the cream sauce.

Add the pasta to the water, return to the boil and cook for 8–10 minutes, or until tender but still firm to the bite. Drain the pasta and transfer to a warmed serving dish.

Add the creamy asparagus sauce and chervil to the pasta and toss lightly. Serve immediately with the Parmesan cheese shavings.

SERVES 4

pinch of saffron threads

2 tbsp hot water

450 g/1 lb asparagus spears

25 g/1 oz butter

1 small onion, finely chopped

2 tbsp dry white wine

225 ml/8 fl oz double cream

grated rind and juice of ½ lemon

115 g/4 oz shelled fresh peas

350 g/12 oz dried tagliatelle

2 tbsp chopped fresh chervil

salt and pepper

fresh Parmesan cheese shavings, to serve

PAPPARDELLE WITH PUMPKIN SAUCE

Melt the butter in a large heavy-based saucepan. Add the shallots, sprinkle with a little salt, cover and cook over a very low heat, stirring occasionally, for 30 minutes.

Add the pumpkin pieces and season to taste with nutmeg. Cover and cook over a very low heat, stirring occasionally, for 40 minutes, or until the pumpkin is pulpy. Stir in the cream, Parmesan cheese and parsley and remove the saucepan from the heat.

Meanwhile, bring a large heavy-based saucepan of lightly salted water to the boil. Add the pasta, return to the boil and cook for 8–10 minutes, or until tender but still firm to the bite. Drain, reserving 2–3 tablespoons of the cooking water.

Add the pasta to the pumpkin mixture and stir in the reserved cooking water if the mixture seems too thick. Cook, stirring, for 1 minute, then transfer to a warmed serving dish and serve immediately with extra grated Parmesan cheese.

SERVES 4

55 g/2 oz butter

6 shallots, very finely chopped

800 g/1 lb 12 oz pumpkin, peeled, deseeded and cut into pieces

pinch of freshly grated nutmeg

200 ml/7 fl oz single cream

4 tbsp freshly grated Parmesan cheese, plus extra to serve

2 tbsp chopped fresh flat-leaf parsley

350 g/12 oz dried pappardelle

salt

PENNE WITH MIXED BEANS

SERVES 4

1 tbsp olive oil

1 onion, chopped

1 garlic clove, finely chopped

1 carrot, finely chopped

1 celery stick, finely chopped

425 g/15 oz canned mixed beans,
   drained and rinsed

225 ml/8 fl oz passata

1 tbsp chopped fresh chervil,
   plus extra leaves to garnish

350 g/12 oz dried penne

salt and pepper

Heat the oil in a large heavy-based frying pan. Add the onion, garlic, carrot and celery and cook over a low heat, stirring occasionally, for 5 minutes, or until the onion has softened.

Add the mixed beans, passata and chopped chervil to the frying pan and season the mixture to taste with salt and pepper. Cover and simmer gently for 15 minutes.

Meanwhile, bring a large heavy-based saucepan of lightly salted water to the boil. Add the pasta, return to the boil and cook for 8–10 minutes, or until tender but still firm to the bite. Drain the pasta and transfer to a warmed serving dish. Add the mixed bean sauce, toss well and serve immediately, garnished with extra chervil.

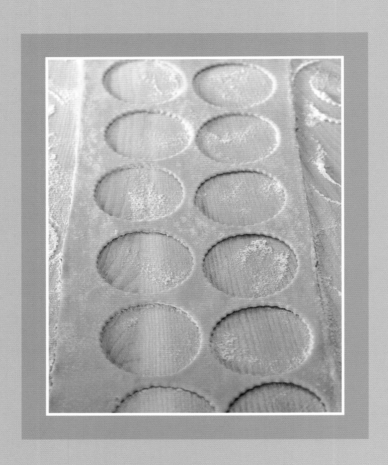

FILLED & BAKED

LASAGNE AL FORNO

Preheat the oven to 190°C/375°F/Gas Mark 5. Heat the oil in a large heavy-based saucepan. Add the pancetta and cook over a medium heat, stirring occasionally, for 3 minutes, or until the fat begins to run. Add the onion and garlic and cook, stirring occasionally, for 5 minutes, or until softened.

Add the beef and cook, breaking it up with a wooden spoon, until browned all over. Stir in the celery and carrots and cook for 5 minutes. Season to taste with salt and pepper. Add the sugar, oregano and tomatoes and their can juices. Bring to the boil, reduce the heat and simmer for 30 minutes.

Meanwhile, to make the cheese sauce, stir the mustard and Cheddar cheese into the Béchamel Sauce.

In a large, rectangular ovenproof dish, make alternate layers of meat sauce, lasagne sheets and Parmesan cheese. Pour the cheese sauce over the layers, covering them completely, and sprinkle with Parmesan cheese. Bake in the preheated oven for 30 minutes, or until golden brown and bubbling. Serve immediately.

SERVES 4

2 tbsp olive oil

55 g/2 oz pancetta, chopped

1 onion, chopped

1 garlic clove, finely chopped

225 g/8 oz fresh beef mince

2 celery sticks, chopped

2 carrots, chopped

pinch of sugar

½ tsp dried oregano

400 g/14 oz canned chopped
    tomatoes

2 tsp Dijon mustard

140 g/5 oz Cheddar cheese, grated

300 ml/10 fl oz Béchamel Sauce
    (see page 13)

225 g/8 oz dried no pre-cook
    lasagne sheets

115 g/4 oz freshly grated
    Parmesan cheese, plus extra for
    sprinkling

salt and pepper

BEEF LASAGNE
WITH RICOTTA &
MOZZARELLA

Heat 100 ml/3½ fl oz of the oil with the butter in a large saucepan. Add the pancetta, onion, celery and carrot and cook over a low heat until softened. Increase the heat to medium, add the beef and cook until evenly browned. Stir in the wine and sun-dried tomato paste, season to taste with salt and pepper and bring to the boil. Reduce the heat, cover and simmer gently, stirring occasionally, for 1½ hours, until the beef is tender.

Meanwhile, heat 2 tablespoons of the remaining oil in a frying pan. Add the sausage and cook for 8–10 minutes. Remove from the pan, remove and discard the skin, then thinly slice.

Transfer the beef to a chopping board and dice finely. Return half the beef to the sauce. Mix the remaining beef with 1 egg, 1 tablespoon of the Parmesan and the breadcrumbs. Shape the mixture into walnut-sized balls. Heat the remaining oil in a frying pan, add the meatballs and cook for 5–8 minutes, until browned.

Pass the ricotta through a sieve into a bowl. Stir in the remaining egg and 4 tablespoons of the remaining Parmesan.

Preheat the oven to 180°C/350°F/Gas Mark 4. In a rectangular ovenproof dish make layers of lasagne sheets, ricotta mixture, meat sauce, meatballs, sausage and mozzarella. Finish with a layer of the ricotta mixture and sprinkle with the remaining Parmesan. Bake in the preheated oven for 20–25 minutes, until golden brown. Serve, garnished with parsley.

SERVES 6

175 ml/6 fl oz olive oil

55 g/2 oz butter

85 g/3 oz pancetta, diced

1 onion, finely chopped

1 celery stick, finely chopped

1 carrot, finely chopped

350 g/12 oz beef topside in a
   single piece

5 tbsp red wine

2 tbsp sun-dried tomato paste

200 g/7 oz Italian sausage

2 eggs

115 g/4 oz Parmesan cheese,
   freshly grated

25 g/1 oz fresh breadcrumbs

350 g/12 oz ricotta cheese

8 sheets no pre-cook lasagne

350 g/12 oz mozzarella cheese,
   sliced

salt and pepper

chopped fresh parsley, to garnish

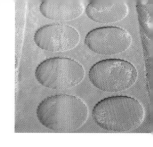

MIXED MEAT LASAGNE

SERVES 6

1 onion, chopped

1 carrot, chopped

1 celery stick, chopped

85 g/3 oz pancetta, chopped

175 g/6 oz fresh beef mince

175 g/6 oz fresh pork mince

3 tbsp olive oil

100 ml/3½ fl oz red wine

150 ml/5 fl oz beef stock

1 tbsp tomato purée

1 bay leaf

1 clove

150 ml/5 fl oz milk

400 g/14 oz dried no pre-cook
   lasagne sheets

600 ml/1 pint Béchamel Sauce
   (see page 13)

140 g/5 oz freshly grated
   Parmesan cheese

140 g/5 oz mozzarella, diced

55 g/2 oz butter, diced

salt and pepper

Mix the onion, carrot, celery, pancetta, beef and pork together in a large bowl. Heat the oil in a large heavy-based frying pan, add the meat mixture and cook over a medium heat, breaking up the meat with a wooden spoon, until it is browned all over. Pour in the wine, then bring to the boil and cook until reduced. Pour in 125 ml/4 fl oz of the stock, bring to the boil and cook until reduced.

Mix the tomato purée and remaining stock together in a small bowl, then add to the frying pan with the bay leaf and clove. Season to taste with salt and pepper and pour in the milk. Cover and simmer for 1 hour.

Preheat the oven to 200°C/400°F/Gas Mark 6. Remove and discard the bay leaf and the clove from the meat sauce. In a large ovenproof dish, make alternate layers of lasagne sheets, meat sauce, Béchamel Sauce, half the Parmesan cheese and the mozzarella. Finish with a layer of Béchamel Sauce and sprinkle with the remaining Parmesan.

Dot the top of the lasagne with butter and bake in the preheated oven for 25 minutes, or until golden brown. Serve immediately.

CHICKEN
LASAGNE

Preheat the oven to 190°C/375°F/Gas Mark 5. Heat the oil in a heavy-based saucepan. Add the chicken and cook over a medium heat, breaking it up with a wooden spoon, for 5 minutes, or until it is browned all over. Add the garlic, carrots and leeks and cook, stirring occasionally, for 5 minutes.

Stir in the stock and tomato purée and season to taste with salt and pepper. Bring to the boil, reduce the heat, cover and simmer for 30 minutes.

Stir half the Cheddar cheese and the mustard into the hot Béchamel Sauce. In a large ovenproof dish, make alternate layers of the chicken mixture, lasagne sheets and cheese sauce, ending with a layer of cheese sauce. Sprinkle with the remaining Cheddar cheese and bake in the preheated oven for 1 hour, or until golden brown and bubbling. Serve immediately.

SERVES 6

2 tbsp olive oil

900 g/2 lb fresh chicken mince

1 garlic clove, finely chopped

4 carrots, chopped

4 leeks, sliced

450 ml/16 fl oz chicken stock

2 tbsp tomato purée

115 g/4 oz Cheddar cheese, grated

1 tsp Dijon mustard

600 ml/1 pint Béchamel Sauce
  (see page 13)

115 g/4 oz dried no pre-cook
  lasagne sheets

salt and pepper

CHICKEN & SPINACH LASAGNE

FILLED & BAKED

250

To make the tomato sauce, put the tomatoes into a pan and stir in the onion, garlic, wine, tomato purée and oregano. Bring to the boil and simmer for 20 minutes, until thick. Season well with salt and pepper.

Preheat the oven to 190°C/375°F/Gas Mark 5. Drain the spinach again and spread it out on kitchen paper to make sure that as much water as possible is removed. Layer the spinach in the base of a large ovenproof baking dish. Sprinkle with ground nutmeg and season to taste with salt and pepper.

Arrange the diced chicken over the spinach and spoon over the tomato sauce. Arrange the sheets of lasagne over the tomato sauce.

Blend the cornflour with a little of the milk to make a paste. Pour the remaining milk into a pan and stir in the paste. Heat, stirring, until the sauce thickens. Season well.

Spoon the sauce over the lasagne sheets and transfer the dish to a baking tray. Sprinkle the grated Parmesan cheese over the sauce and bake in the preheated oven for 25 minutes until golden, then serve.

SERVES 4

350 g/12 oz frozen chopped spinach, thawed and drained

½ tsp freshly grated nutmeg

450 g/1 lb lean, cooked chicken, skinned and diced

4 sheets dried no pre-cook lasagne verde

1½ tbsp cornflour

425 ml/15 fl oz milk

70 g/2½ oz freshly grated Parmesan cheese

salt and pepper

tomato sauce

400 g/14 oz canned chopped tomatoes

1 onion, finely chopped

1 garlic clove, crushed

150 ml/5 fl oz white wine

3 tbsp tomato purée

1 tsp dried oregano

salt and pepper

CHICKEN & MUSHROOM LASAGNE

SERVES 4

14 dried no pre-cook lasagne
   sheets

850 ml/1½ pints Béchamel Sauce
   (see page 13)

85 g/3 oz grated Parmesan cheese

wild mushroom sauce

2 tbsp olive oil

2 garlic cloves, crushed

1 large onion, finely chopped

225 g/8 oz wild mushrooms,
   sliced

300 g/10½ oz fresh chicken mince

85 g/3 oz chicken livers, finely
   chopped

115 g/4 oz Parma ham, diced

150 ml/5 fl oz Marsala

280 g/10 oz canned chopped
   tomatoes

1 tbsp chopped fresh basil leaves

2 tbsp tomato purée

salt and pepper

Preheat the oven to 190°C/375°F/Gas Mark 5. To make the sauce, heat the oil in a large heavy-based saucepan. Add the garlic, onion and mushrooms and cook, stirring frequently, for 6 minutes. Add the chicken mince, chicken livers and Parma ham and cook over a low heat for 12 minutes, or until the meat has browned.

Stir the Marsala, tomatoes, basil and tomato purée into the mixture and cook for 4 minutes. Season to taste with salt and pepper, cover and leave to simmer for 30 minutes. Uncover, stir and simmer for a further 15 minutes.

Arrange sheets of lasagne over the base of an ovenproof dish, spoon over a layer of the mushroom sauce, then spoon over a layer of Béchamel Sauce. Place another layer of lasagne on top and repeat the process twice, finishing with a layer of Béchamel Sauce. Sprinkle over the grated Parmesan cheese and bake in the preheated oven for 35 minutes, or until golden brown and bubbling. Serve immediately.

LASAGNE ALLA MARINARA

Preheat the oven to 190°C/375°F/Gas Mark 5. Melt the butter in a large heavy-based saucepan. Add the prawns and monkfish and cook over a medium heat for 3–5 minutes, or until the prawns change colour. Transfer the prawns to a small heatproof bowl with a slotted spoon. Add the mushrooms to the saucepan and cook, stirring occasionally, for 5 minutes. Transfer the fish and mushrooms to the bowl.

Stir the fish mixture, with any juices, into the Béchamel Sauce and season to taste with salt and pepper. Layer the tomatoes, chervil, basil, Béchamel Sauce mixture and lasagne sheets in a large ovenproof dish, ending with a layer of the fish mixture. Sprinkle evenly with the grated Parmesan cheese.

Bake in the preheated oven for 35 minutes, or until golden brown, then serve immediately.

SERVES 6

15 g/½ oz butter

225 g/8 oz raw prawns, peeled and deveined

450 g/1 lb monkfish fillets, skinned and chopped

225 g/8 oz chestnut mushrooms, chopped

850 ml/1½ pints Béchamel Sauce (see page 13)

400 g/14 oz canned chopped tomatoes

1 tbsp chopped fresh chervil

1 tbsp shredded fresh basil

175 g/6 oz dried no pre-cook lasagne sheets

85 g/3 oz freshly grated Parmesan cheese

salt and pepper

SALMON LASAGNE ROLLS

Cook the lasagne in a large pan of boiling water for 6 minutes, or according to the instructions on the packet. Remove with tongs and drain on a clean tea towel.

Melt half the butter in a saucepan. Add the onion and cook over a low heat, stirring occasionally, for 5 minutes, until softened. Add the red pepper, courgette and ginger and cook, stirring occasionally, for 10 minutes. Add the mushrooms and salmon and cook for 2 minutes, then mix together the sherry and cornflour and stir into the pan. Cook for a further 4 minutes, until the fish is opaque and flakes easily. Season to taste with salt and pepper and remove the pan from the heat.

Preheat the oven to 200°C/400°F/Gas Mark 6. Brush an ovenproof dish with oil.

Melt the remaining butter in another pan. Stir in the flour and cook, stirring constantly, for 2 minutes. Gradually stir in the milk, then cook, stirring constantly, for 10 minutes. Remove the pan from the heat, stir in half the Cheddar cheese and season to taste with salt and pepper.

Spoon the salmon filling along one of the shorter sides of each sheet of lasagne. Roll up and place in the prepared dish. Pour the sauce over the rolls and sprinkle with the breadcrumbs and remaining cheese. Bake for 15–20 minutes, until the topping is golden and bubbling. Serve immediately with salad leaves.

SERVES 4

8 sheets dried lasagne verde

25 g/1 oz butter

1 onion, sliced

½ red pepper, deseeded and chopped

1 courgette, diced

1 tsp chopped fresh ginger

125 g/4½ oz oyster mushrooms, torn into pieces

225 g/8 oz salmon fillet, skinned and cut into chunks

3 tbsp dry sherry

2 tsp cornflour

vegetable oil, for brushing

3 tbsp plain flour

425 ml/15 fl oz milk

25 g/1 oz finely grated Cheddar cheese

1 tbsp fresh white breadcrumbs

salt and pepper

salad leaves, to serve

VEGETABLE LASAGNE

SERVES 4

olive oil, for brushing

2 aubergines, sliced

25 g/1 oz butter

1 garlic clove, finely chopped

4 courgettes, sliced

1 tbsp finely chopped fresh
flat-leaf parsley

1 tbsp finely chopped fresh
marjoram

225 g/8 oz mozzarella cheese,
grated

600 ml/1 pint passata

175 g/6 oz dried no pre-cook
lasagne sheets

600 ml/1 pint Béchamel Sauce
(see page 13)

55 g/2 oz freshly grated Parmesan
cheese

salt and pepper

Preheat the oven to 200°C/400°F/Gas Mark 6. Brush a large
ovenproof dish with oil. Brush a large griddle pan with oil and
heat until smoking. Add half the aubergines and cook over
a medium heat for 8 minutes, or until golden brown all over.
Remove from the griddle pan and drain on kitchen paper. Add the
remaining aubergine slices and extra oil, if necessary, and cook
for 8 minutes, or until golden brown all over.

Melt the butter in a frying pan and add the garlic, courgettes,
parsley and marjoram. Cook over a medium heat, stirring
frequently, for 5 minutes, or until the courgettes are golden
brown all over. Remove from the frying pan and leave to drain
on kitchen paper.

Layer the aubergines, courgettes, mozzarella, passata and
lasagne sheets in the dish, seasoning to taste with salt and
pepper as you go and finishing with a layer of lasagne. Pour
over the Béchamel Sauce, making sure that all the pasta is
covered. Sprinkle with the grated Parmesan cheese and bake in
the preheated oven for 30–40 minutes, or until golden brown.
Serve immediately.

SPINACH & MUSHROOM LASAGNE

Preheat the oven to 200°C/400°F/Gas Mark 6. Lightly grease an ovenproof dish with a little butter.

Melt 55 g/2 oz of the butter in a pan over a low heat. Add the garlic, shallots and wild mushrooms and cook for 3 minutes. Stir in the spinach, 225 g/8 oz of the Cheddar cheese, the nutmeg and chopped basil. Season well with salt and pepper and reserve.

Melt the remaining butter in another pan over a low heat. Add the flour and cook, stirring constantly, for 1 minute. Gradually stir in the hot milk, whisking constantly until smooth. Stir in 25 g/1 oz of the remaining cheese and season to taste with salt and pepper.

Spread half of the mushroom and spinach mixture over the base of the prepared dish. Cover with a layer of lasagne, then with half the cheese sauce. Repeat the process and sprinkle over the remaining cheese. Bake in the preheated oven for 30 minutes, or until golden brown. Serve immediately.

SERVES 4

115 g/4 oz butter, plus extra for greasing

2 garlic cloves, finely chopped

115 g/4 oz shallots

225 g/8 oz wild mushrooms

450 g/1 lb spinach, cooked, drained and finely chopped

280 g/10 oz freshly grated Cheddar cheese

¼ tsp freshly grated nutmeg

1 tsp chopped fresh basil

55 g/2 oz plain flour

600 ml/1 pint hot milk

8 dried no pre-cook lasagne sheets

salt and pepper

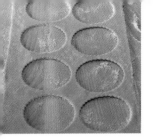

CANNELLONI WITH HAM & RICOTTA

Preheat the oven to 180°C/350°F/Gas Mark 4. Heat the oil in a large heavy-based frying pan. Add the onions and garlic and cook over a low heat, stirring occasionally, for 5 minutes, or until the onion is softened. Add the basil, tomatoes and their can juices and tomato purée and season to taste with salt and pepper. Reduce the heat and simmer for 30 minutes, or until thickened.

Meanwhile, bring a large heavy-based saucepan of lightly salted water to the boil. Add the cannelloni tubes, return to the boil and cook for 8–10 minutes, or until tender but still firm to the bite. Using a slotted spoon, transfer the cannelloni tubes to a large plate and pat dry with kitchen paper.

Grease a large, shallow ovenproof dish with butter. Mix the ricotta, ham and egg together in a bowl and season to taste with salt and pepper. Using a teaspoon, fill the cannelloni tubes with the ricotta mixture and place in a single layer in the dish. Pour the tomato sauce over the cannelloni and sprinkle with the grated pecorino cheese. Bake in the preheated oven for 30 minutes, or until golden brown. Serve immediately.

SERVES 4

2 tbsp olive oil

2 onions, chopped

2 garlic cloves, finely chopped

1 tbsp shredded fresh basil

800 g/1 lb 12 oz canned chopped tomatoes

1 tbsp tomato purée

10–12 dried cannelloni tubes

butter, for greasing

225 g/8 oz ricotta cheese

115 g/4 oz cooked ham, diced

1 egg

55 g/2 oz freshly grated pecorino cheese

salt and pepper

CHICKEN & MUSHROOM CANNELLONI

SERVES 4

butter, for greasing

2 tbsp olive oil

2 garlic cloves, crushed

1 large onion, finely chopped

225 g/8 oz wild mushrooms, sliced

350 g/12 oz fresh chicken mince

115 g/4 oz prosciutto, diced

150 ml/5 fl oz Marsala

200 g/7 oz canned chopped tomatoes

1 tbsp shredded fresh basil leaves

2 tbsp tomato purée

10–12 dried cannelloni tubes

600 ml/1 pint Béchamel Sauce (see page 13)

85 g/3 oz freshly grated Parmesan cheese

salt and pepper

Preheat the oven to 190°C/375°F/Gas Mark 5. Lightly grease a large ovenproof dish. Heat the oil in a heavy-based frying pan. Add the garlic, onion and mushrooms and cook over a low heat, stirring frequently, for 8–10 minutes. Add the chicken mince and prosciutto and cook, stirring frequently, for 12 minutes, or until browned all over. Stir in the Marsala, tomatoes and their can juices, basil and tomato purée and cook for 4 minutes. Season to taste with salt and pepper, then cover and simmer for 30 minutes. Uncover, stir and simmer for 15 minutes.

Meanwhile, bring a large heavy-based saucepan of lightly salted water to the boil. Add the cannelloni tubes, return to the boil and cook for 8–10 minutes, or until tender but still firm to the bite. Using a slotted spoon, transfer the cannelloni tubes to a plate and pat dry with kitchen paper.

Using a teaspoon, fill the cannelloni tubes with the chicken and mushroom mixture. Transfer them to the dish. Pour the Béchamel Sauce over them to cover completely and sprinkle with the grated Parmesan cheese.

Bake in the preheated oven for 30 minutes, or until golden brown and bubbling. Serve immediately.

MUSHROOM CANNELLONI

Preheat the oven to 190°C/375°F/Gas Mark 5. Bring a large saucepan of lightly salted water to the boil. Add the cannelloni tubes, return to the boil and cook for 8–10 minutes, or until tender but still firm to the bite. With a slotted spoon, transfer the cannelloni tubes to a plate and pat dry. Brush a large ovenproof dish with oil.

Heat 2 tablespoons of the oil in a frying pan, add the onion and half the garlic and cook over a low heat for 5 minutes, or until softened. Add the tomatoes and their can juices, tomato purée and olives and season to taste with salt and pepper. Bring to the boil and cook for 3–4 minutes. Pour the sauce into the ovenproof dish.

To make the filling, melt the butter in a heavy-based frying pan. Add the mushrooms and remaining garlic and cook over a medium heat, stirring frequently, for 3–5 minutes, or until tender. Remove the frying pan from the heat. Mix the breadcrumbs, milk and remaining oil together in a large bowl, then stir in the ricotta, the mushroom mixture and 4 tablespoons of the Parmesan cheese. Season to taste with salt and pepper.

Fill the cannelloni tubes with the mushroom mixture and place them in the prepared dish. Brush with oil and sprinkle with the remaining Parmesan cheese, the pine kernels and almonds. Bake in the preheated oven for 25 minutes, or until golden.

SERVES 4

12 dried cannelloni tubes

6 tbsp olive oil, plus extra for brushing

1 onion, finely chopped

2 garlic cloves, finely chopped

800 g/1 lb 12 oz canned chopped tomatoes

1 tbsp tomato purée

8 black olives, stoned and chopped

25 g/1 oz butter

450 g/1 lb wild mushrooms, finely chopped

85 g/3 oz fresh breadcrumbs

150 ml/5 fl oz milk

225 g/8 oz ricotta cheese

6 tbsp freshly grated Parmesan cheese

2 tbsp pine kernels

2 tbsp flaked almonds

salt and pepper

BROCCOLI & MASCARPONE CANNELLONI

Preheat the oven to 190°C/375°F/Gas Mark 5. Bring a large heavy-based saucepan of lightly salted water to the boil. Add the cannelloni tubes, return to the boil and cook for 8–10 minutes, or until tender but still firm to the bite. Transfer the pasta to a plate and pat dry with kitchen paper. Brush a large ovenproof dish with oil.

Heat 2 tablespoons of the oil in a frying pan. Add the shallots and garlic and cook over a low heat for 5 minutes, or until softened. Add the tomatoes, peppers and sun-dried tomato paste and season to taste with salt and pepper. Bring to the boil, then reduce the heat and simmer for 20 minutes. Stir in the basil and pour the sauce into the dish.

While the sauce is cooking, place the broccoli in a saucepan of lightly salted boiling water and cook for 10 minutes, or until tender. Drain, then process to a purée in a food processor.

Mix the breadcrumbs, milk and remaining oil together in a large bowl, then stir in the mascarpone cheese, nutmeg, broccoli purée and 4 tablespoons of the pecorino cheese. Season to taste with salt and pepper.

Fill the cannelloni tubes with the broccoli mixture and place them in the prepared dish. Brush with oil and sprinkle with the remaining pecorino cheese and the almonds. Bake in the preheated oven for 25 minutes, or until golden.

SERVES 4

12 dried cannelloni tubes

6 tbsp olive oil, plus extra for brushing

4 shallots, finely chopped

1 garlic clove, finely chopped

600 g/1 lb 5 oz plum tomatoes, peeled, deseeded and chopped

3 red peppers, deseeded and chopped

1 tbsp sun-dried tomato paste

1 tbsp shredded fresh basil leaves

1 lb/450 g broccoli, broken into florets

85 g/3 oz fresh breadcrumbs

150 ml/5 fl oz milk

225 g/8 oz mascarpone cheese

pinch of freshly grated nutmeg

6 tbsp freshly grated pecorino cheese

2 tbsp flaked almonds

salt and pepper

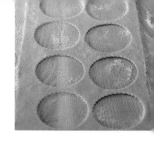

VEGETABLE CANNELLONI

SERVES 4

12 dried cannelloni tubes

1 aubergine

125 ml/4 fl oz olive oil, plus extra
  for brushing

225 g/8 oz spinach

2 garlic cloves, crushed

1 tsp ground cumin

85 g/3 oz mushrooms, chopped

55 g/2 oz mozzarella cheese,
  sliced

salt and pepper

lamb's lettuce, to garnish

tomato sauce

1 tbsp olive oil

1 onion, chopped

2 garlic cloves, crushed

800 g/1 lb 12 oz canned chopped
  tomatoes

1 tsp caster sugar

2 tbsp chopped fresh basil

Preheat the oven to 190°C/375°F/Gas Mark 5. Bring a large
heavy-bottom saucepan of lightly salted water to the boil. Add
the cannelloni tubes, return to the boil and cook for 8–10 minutes,
or until tender but still firm to the bite. Transfer the pasta to a
plate and pat dry with kitchen paper. Brush a large ovenproof dish
with oil.

Cut the aubergine into small dice. Heat the oil in a frying
pan over a medium heat. Add the aubergine and cook, stirring
frequently, for about 2–3 minutes.

Add the spinach, garlic, cumin and mushrooms and reduce the
heat. Season to taste with salt and pepper and cook, stirring, for
about 2–3 minutes. Spoon the mixture into the cannelloni tubes
and put into the dish in a single layer.

To make the sauce, heat the oil in a pan over a medium
heat. Add the onion and garlic and cook for 1 minute. Add the
tomatoes, sugar and basil and bring to the boil. Reduce the
heat and simmer for about 5 minutes. Spoon the sauce over
the cannelloni tubes.

Arrange the mozzarella cheese on top of the sauce and bake in
the preheated oven for about 30 minutes, or until the cheese is
golden brown and bubbling. Serve garnished with lamb's lettuce.

HOT TOMATO & CONCHIGLIE GRATIN

Put the onion, tomatoes and milk in a large heavy-based saucepan and bring just to the boil. Add the chillies, garlic, coriander and pasta, season to taste with salt and pepper and cook over a medium heat, stirring frequently, for 2–3 minutes.

Add just enough water to cover and cook, stirring frequently, for 8–10 minutes, until the pasta is tender but still firm to the bite. Meanwhile, preheat the grill.

Spoon the pasta mixture into individual flameproof dishes and sprinkle evenly with the cheese. Place under the grill for 3–4 minutes, until the cheese has melted. Serve immediately.

SERVES 4

1 onion, chopped

400 g/14 oz canned chopped tomatoes

225 ml/8 fl oz milk

1–2 red chillies, deseeded and finely chopped

1 garlic clove, finely chopped

pinch of ground coriander

280 g/10 oz dried conchiglie

85 g/3 oz Gruyère cheese, grated

salt and pepper

BEEF & MACARONI SOUFFLÉ

Preheat the oven to 190°C/375°F/Gas Mark 5. Heat the oil in a large heavy-based frying pan. Add the onion and cook over a low heat, stirring occasionally, for 5 minutes, or until softened. Add the beef and cook, breaking up the meat with a wooden spoon, until browned. Stir in the garlic, tomatoes and their can juices and tomato purée, then season to taste with salt and pepper. Bring to the boil, reduce the heat and simmer for 20 minutes, then remove the frying pan from the heat and leave to cool slightly.

Meanwhile, bring a large heavy-based saucepan of lightly salted water to the boil. Add the pasta, return to the boil and cook for 8–10 minutes, or until tender but still firm to the bite. Drain and reserve.

Lightly grease a 1.5-litre/2¾-pint soufflé dish with butter. Beat the egg yolks and add them to the meat sauce, then stir in the pasta. Whisk the egg whites until stiff peaks form, then fold into the sauce. Spoon the mixture into the dish, sprinkle with the grated Parmesan cheese and bake in the preheated oven for 45 minutes, or until well risen and golden brown. Sprinkle with extra grated Parmesan cheese and serve immediately.

SERVES 4

2 tbsp olive oil

1 large onion, chopped

225 g/8 oz fresh beef mince

1 garlic clove, finely chopped

400 g/14 oz canned chopped tomatoes

1 tbsp tomato purée

175 g/6 oz dried macaroni

butter, for greasing

3 eggs, separated

40 g/1½ oz freshly grated Parmesan cheese, plus extra to serve

salt and pepper

SICILIAN LINGUINE

SERVES 4

125 ml/4 fl oz olive oil, plus extra
for brushing

2 aubergines, sliced

350 g/12 oz fresh beef mince

1 onion, chopped

2 garlic cloves, finely chopped

2 tbsp tomato purée

400 g/14 oz canned chopped
tomatoes

1 tsp Worcestershire sauce

1 tbsp chopped fresh flat-leaf
parsley

55 g/2 oz stoned black olives,
sliced

1 red pepper, deseeded and
chopped

175 g/6 oz dried linguine

115 g/4 oz freshly grated
Parmesan cheese

salt and pepper

Preheat the oven to 200°C/400°F/Gas Mark 6. Brush a 20-cm/
8-inch loose-based round cake tin with oil and line the base
with baking paper. Heat half the oil in a frying pan. Add the
aubergines in batches, and cook until lightly browned on both
sides. Add more oil, as required. Drain the aubergines on kitchen
paper, then arrange in overlapping slices to cover the base and
sides of the cake tin, reserving a few slices.

Heat the remaining oil in a large saucepan and add the beef,
onion and garlic. Cook over a medium heat, breaking up the
meat with a wooden spoon, until browned all over. Add the
tomato purée, tomatoes and their can juices, Worcestershire
sauce and parsley. Season to taste with salt and pepper and
simmer for 10 minutes. Add the olives and red pepper and cook
for a further 10 minutes.

Meanwhile, bring a saucepan of lightly salted water to the boil.
Add the pasta, return to the boil and cook for 8–10 minutes, or
until tender but still firm to the bite. Drain and transfer to a bowl.
Add the meat sauce and Parmesan and toss, then spoon into
the cake tin, press down and cover with the remaining aubergine
slices. Bake in the preheated oven for 40 minutes. Leave to stand
for 5 minutes, then loosen around the edges and invert on to a
plate. Remove and discard the baking paper and serve.

PORK & PASTA BAKE

Preheat the oven to 200°C/400°F/Gas Mark 6. Heat the oil in a large heavy-based frying pan. Add the onion, garlic and carrots and cook over a low heat, stirring occasionally, for 5 minutes, or until the onion has softened. Add the pancetta and cook for 5 minutes. Add the chopped mushrooms and cook, stirring occasionally, for a further 2 minutes. Add the pork and cook, breaking it up with a wooden spoon, until the meat is browned all over. Stir in the wine, passata, chopped tomatoes and their can juices and chopped sage. Season to taste with salt and pepper, bring to the boil, then cover and simmer over a low heat for 25–30 minutes.

Meanwhile, bring a large heavy-based saucepan of lightly salted water to the boil. Add the pasta, return to the boil and cook for 8–10 minutes, or until tender but still firm to the bite.

Spoon the pork mixture into a large ovenproof dish. Stir the mozzarella cheese and half the Parmesan cheese into the Béchamel Sauce. Drain the pasta and stir the sauce into it, then spoon it over the pork mixture. Sprinkle with the remaining Parmesan cheese and bake in the preheated oven for 25–30 minutes, or until golden brown. Serve immediately, garnished with sage sprigs.

SERVES 4

2 tbsp olive oil

1 onion, chopped

1 garlic clove, finely chopped

2 carrots, diced

55 g/2 oz pancetta, chopped

115 g/4 oz mushrooms, chopped

450 g/1 lb fresh pork mince

125 ml/4 fl oz dry white wine

4 tbsp passata

200 g/7 oz canned chopped tomatoes

2 tsp chopped fresh sage, plus extra sprigs to garnish

225 g/8 oz dried penne

140 g/5 oz mozzarella cheese, diced

4 tbsp freshly grated Parmesan

300 ml/10 fl oz Béchamel Sauce (see page 13)

salt and pepper

PASTICCIO

Preheat the oven to 190°C/375°F/Gas Mark 5. Heat the oil in a large heavy-based frying pan. Add the onion and garlic and cook over a low heat, stirring occasionally, for 5 minutes, or until softened. Add the lamb and cook, breaking it up with a wooden spoon, until browned all over. Add the tomato purée and sprinkle in the flour. Cook, stirring, for 1 minute, then stir in the stock. Season to taste with salt and pepper and stir in the cinnamon. Bring to the boil, reduce the heat, cover and cook for 25 minutes.

Meanwhile, bring a large heavy-based saucepan of lightly salted water to the boil. Add the pasta, return to the boil and cook for 8–10 minutes, or until tender but still firm to the bite.

Drain the pasta and stir into the lamb mixture. Spoon into a large ovenproof dish and arrange the tomato slices on top. Beat together the yogurt and eggs then spoon over the lamb evenly. Bake in the preheated oven for 1 hour. Serve immediately.

SERVES 4

1 tbsp olive oil

1 onion, chopped

2 garlic cloves, finely chopped

450 g/1 lb fresh lamb mince

2 tbsp tomato purée

2 tbsp plain flour

300 ml/10 fl oz chicken stock

1 tsp ground cinnamon

115 g/4 oz dried macaroni

2 beef tomatoes, sliced

300 ml/10 fl oz Greek yogurt

2 eggs, lightly beaten

salt and pepper

BEAN & PASTA BAKE

SERVES 4

225 g/8 oz dried haricot beans,
  soaked overnight and drained

225 g/8 oz dried penne

6 tbsp olive oil

850 ml/1½ pints vegetable stock

2 large onions, sliced

2 garlic cloves, chopped

2 bay leaves

1 tsp dried oregano

1 tsp dried thyme

5 tbsp red wine

2 tbsp tomato purée

2 celery sticks, sliced

1 fennel bulb, sliced

115 g/4 oz mushrooms, sliced

225 g/8 oz tomatoes, sliced

1 tsp dark muscovado sugar

55 g/2 oz dry white breadcrumbs

salt and pepper

crusty bread, to serve

Preheat the oven to 180°C/350°F/Gas Mark 4. Put the beans in a large pan, add water to cover and bring to the boil. Boil the beans rapidly for 20 minutes, then drain them and set aside.

Cook the pasta for 3 minutes in a large saucepan of boiling salted water, adding 1 tablespoon of the oil. Drain in a colander and set aside.

Put the beans in a large flameproof casserole, pour in the stock and stir in the remaining oil, the onions, garlic, bay leaves, herbs, wine and tomato purée. Bring to the boil, cover the casserole and cook in the preheated oven for 2 hours.

Remove the casserole from the oven and add the reserved pasta, the celery, fennel, mushrooms and tomatoes and season to taste with salt and pepper. Stir in the sugar and sprinkle the breadcrumbs on top. Cover the casserole again, return to the oven and continue cooking for 1 hour. Serve with crusty bread.

BAKED TUNA
& RICOTTA
RIGATONI

Preheat the oven to 200°C/400°F/Gas Mark 6. Lightly grease a large ovenproof dish with butter. Bring a large heavy-based saucepan of lightly salted water to the boil. Add the rigatoni, return to the boil and cook for 8–10 minutes, or until just tender but still firm to the bite. Drain the pasta and leave until cool enough to handle.

Meanwhile, mix the tuna and ricotta cheese together in a bowl to form a soft paste. Spoon the mixture into a piping bag and use to fill the rigatoni. Arrange the filled pasta tubes side by side in the prepared dish.

To make the sauce, mix the cream and Parmesan cheese together in a bowl and season to taste with salt and pepper. Spoon the sauce over the rigatoni and top with the sun-dried tomatoes, arranged in a criss-cross pattern. Bake in the preheated oven for 20 minutes. Serve hot straight from the dish.

SERVES 4

butter, for greasing

450 g/1 lb dried rigatoni

200 g/7 oz canned flaked tuna, drained

225 g/8 oz ricotta cheese

125 ml/4 fl oz double cream

225 g/8 oz freshly grated Parmesan cheese

115 g/4 oz sun-dried tomatoes, drained and sliced

salt and pepper

LAYERED SALMON & PRAWN SPAGHETTI

Preheat the oven to 180°C/350°F/Gas Mark 4. Butter a large ovenproof dish and set aside.

Bring a large saucepan of lightly salted water to the boil. Add the pasta, bring back to the boil and cook for 8–10 minutes, until tender but still firm to the bite. Drain well, return to the saucepan, add 55 g/2 oz of the butter and toss well.

Spoon half the spaghetti into the prepared dish, cover with the strips of smoked salmon, then top with the prawns. Pour over half the Béchamel Sauce and sprinkle with half the Parmesan cheese. Add the remaining spaghetti, cover with the remaining sauce and sprinkle with the remaining Parmesan cheese. Dice the remaining butter and dot it over the surface.

Bake in the preheated oven for 15 minutes, until the top is golden. Serve immediately, garnished with rocket.

SERVES 6

350 g/12 oz dried spaghetti

70 g/2½ oz butter, plus extra for greasing

200 g/7 oz smoked salmon, cut into strips

280 g/10 oz large cooked prawns, peeled and deveined

300 ml/10 fl oz Béchamel Sauce (see page 13)

115 g/4 oz freshly grated Parmesan cheese

salt

rocket, to garnish

MACARONI & SEAFOOD BAKE

SERVES 4

350 g/12 oz dried macaroni

85 g/3 oz butter, plus extra for greasing

2 small fennel bulbs, trimmed and thinly sliced

175 g/6 oz mushrooms, thinly sliced

175 g/6 oz cooked peeled prawns

pinch of cayenne pepper

600 ml/1 pint Béchamel Sauce (see page 13)

55 g/2 oz freshly grated Parmesan cheese

2 large tomatoes, halved and sliced

olive oil, for brushing

1 tsp dried oregano

salt

Preheat the oven to 180°C/350°F/Gas Mark 4. Bring a large saucepan of lightly salted water to the boil. Add the pasta, return to the boil and cook for 8–10 minutes, or until tender but still firm to the bite. Drain and return to the saucepan. Add 25 g/1 oz of the butter to the pasta, cover, shake the saucepan and keep warm.

Melt the remaining butter in a separate saucepan. Add the fennel and cook for 3–4 minutes. Stir in the mushrooms and cook for a further 2 minutes. Stir in the prawns, then remove the saucepan from the heat.

Stir the cooked pasta, cayenne pepper and prawn mixture into the Béchamel Sauce.

Grease a large ovenproof dish, then pour the mixture into the dish and spread evenly. Sprinkle over the Parmesan cheese and arrange the tomato slices in a ring around the edge. Brush the tomatoes with oil, then sprinkle over the oregano. Bake in the preheated oven for 25 minutes, or until golden brown. Serve immediately.

MACARONI & TUNA BAKE

Preheat the oven to 200°C/400°F/Gas Mark 6. Bring a large saucepan of lightly salted water to the boil. Add the macaroni, return to the boil and cook for 8–10 minutes, or until tender but still firm to the bite. Drain, rinse and drain thoroughly.

Heat the oil in a frying pan and cook the garlic, mushrooms and red pepper until soft. Add the tuna and oregano, and season to taste with salt and pepper. Heat through.

Grease a 1-litre/1¾-pint ovenproof dish with a little butter. Add half of the cooked macaroni, cover with the tuna mixture, then add the remaining macaroni.

Melt the butter in a saucepan, stir in the flour and cook for 1 minute. Add the milk gradually and bring to the boil. Simmer for 1–2 minutes, stirring constantly, until thickened. Season to taste with salt and pepper. Pour the sauce over the macaroni. Lay the sliced tomatoes over the sauce and sprinkle with the breadcrumbs and cheese. Cook in the preheated oven for 25 minutes, or until piping hot and the top is well browned.

SERVES 2

140 g/5 oz dried macaroni

1 tbsp olive oil

1 garlic clove, crushed

55 g/2 oz button mushrooms, sliced

½ red pepper, deseeded and thinly sliced

200 g/7 oz canned tuna in brine, drained and flaked

½ tsp dried oregano

25 g/1 oz butter or margarine, plus extra for greasing

1 tbsp plain flour

250 ml/9 fl oz milk

2 tomatoes, sliced

2 tbsp dried breadcrumbs

25 g/1 oz mature Cheddar or Parmesan cheese, grated

salt and pepper

MACARONI CHEESE & TOMATO

Preheat the oven to 190°C/375°F/Gas Mark 5. Grease a deep ovenproof dish with a little butter.

To make the tomato sauce, heat the oil in a pan over a medium heat. Add the shallot and garlic and cook, stirring constantly, for 1 minute. Add the tomatoes and basil and season to taste with salt and pepper. Cook, stirring, for 10 minutes.

Meanwhile, bring a large pan of lightly salted water to the boil over a medium heat. Add the macaroni and cook for 8–10 minutes, or until tender but still firm to the bite. Drain well.

Mix the grated Cheddar and Parmesan cheeses together in a small bowl. Spoon one third of the tomato sauce into the base of the prepared dish, then cover with one third of the macaroni and top with one third of the mixed cheeses. Season to taste with salt and pepper. Repeat these layers twice, ending with a layer of the grated cheeses.

Mix the breadcrumbs and basil together and sprinkle evenly over the top. Dot the topping with the butter and cook in the preheated oven for about 25 minutes, or until the topping is golden brown and bubbling. Serve.

SERVES 4

225 g/8 oz dried macaroni

175 g/6 oz freshly grated Cheddar cheese

100 g/3½ oz freshly grated Parmesan cheese

4 tbsp fresh white breadcrumbs

1 tbsp chopped fresh basil

1 tbsp butter or margarine, plus extra for greasing

salt and pepper

tomato sauce

1 tbsp olive oil

1 shallot, finely chopped

2 garlic cloves, crushed

500 g/1 lb 2 oz canned chopped tomatoes

1 tbsp chopped fresh basil

salt and pepper

MACARONI & THREE CHEESES

SERVES 4

butter, for greasing

225 g/8 oz dried macaroni

1 egg, beaten

125 g/4½ oz freshly grated
   Cheddar cheese

1 tbsp wholegrain mustard

2 tbsp snipped fresh chives, plus
   extra to garnish

600 ml/1 pint Béchamel Sauce
   (see page 13)

4 tomatoes, sliced

125 g/4½ oz freshly grated
   Gruyère cheese

55 g/2 oz freshly grated blue
   cheese

2 tbsp sunflower seeds

salt and pepper

Preheat the oven to 190°C/375°F/Gas Mark 5. Lightly grease a
large ovenproof dish with a little butter.

Bring a pan of lightly salted water to the boil over a medium
heat. Add the macaroni, bring back to the boil and cook for
8–10 minutes, or until tender but still firm to the bite. Drain and
put into the prepared dish.

Stir the beaten egg, Cheddar cheese, mustard and chives into
the Béchamel Sauce and season to taste with salt and pepper.

Spoon the sauce over the macaroni, making sure it is well
covered. Arrange the sliced tomatoes in a layer over the top.

Sprinkle the Gruyère and blue cheeses and the sunflower seeds
evenly over the top. Put the dish onto a baking tray and bake in
the preheated oven for 25–30 minutes, or until the topping is
golden and bubbling.

Garnish with snipped chives and serve immediately.

MIXED
VEGETABLE
AGNOLOTTI

To make the filling, heat the oil in a large heavy-based saucepan. Add the onion and garlic and cook over a low heat, stirring occasionally, for 5 minutes, or until softened. Add the aubergines, courgettes, tomatoes, green and red peppers, sun-dried tomato paste and basil. Season to taste with salt and pepper, cover and simmer gently, stirring occasionally, for 20 minutes.

Lightly grease an ovenproof dish with butter. Roll out the pasta dough on a lightly floured work surface and stamp out 7.5-cm/ 3-inch rounds with a fluted biscuit cutter. Place a spoonful of the vegetable filling on each round. Dampen the edges slightly and fold the pasta rounds over, pressing together to seal. Place on a floured tea towel and leave to stand for 1 hour. Preheat the oven to 200°C/400°F/Gas Mark 6.

Bring a large saucepan of lightly salted water to the boil. Add the agnolotti, in batches if necessary, return to the boil and cook for 3–4 minutes. Remove with a slotted spoon, drain and transfer to the prepared dish. Sprinkle with the Parmesan cheese and bake in the preheated oven for 20 minutes. Serve immediately.

SERVES 4

butter, for greasing

1 quantity Basic Pasta Dough (see page 8)

plain flour, for dusting

85 g/3 oz freshly grated Parmesan

salt

filling

125 ml/4 fl oz olive oil

1 red onion, chopped

3 garlic cloves, chopped

2 large aubergines, cut into chunks

3 large courgettes, cut into chunks

6 beef tomatoes, peeled, deseeded and roughly chopped

1 large green pepper, deseeded and diced

1 large red pepper, deseeded and diced

1 tbsp sun-dried tomato paste

1 tbsp shredded fresh basil

salt and pepper

PUMPKIN & RICOTTA RAVIOLI

Preheat the oven to 200°C/400°F/Gas Mark 6. Place the unpeeled garlic cloves on a baking sheet and bake for 10 minutes. Meanwhile, put the pumpkin in a steamer set over a pan of boiling water. Cover and steam for 15 minutes, until tender.

Chop the sun-dried tomatoes. Squeeze the garlic cloves out of their skins into a bowl. Add the pumpkin, sun-dried tomatoes, ricotta and rosemary and mash well with a potato masher until thoroughly combined. Season to taste with salt and pepper and leave to cool.

Divide the pasta dough in half and wrap 1 piece in clingfilm. Roll out the other piece on a lightly floured surface to a rectangle 2–3 mm/1⁄16–1⁄8 inch thick. Cover with a damp tea towel and roll out the other piece of dough to the same size. Place small mounds, about 1 teaspoon each, of the pumpkin filling in rows 4 cm/1½ inches apart on a sheet of pasta dough. Brush the spaces between the mounds with beaten egg. Lift the second sheet of dough on top and press down firmly between the pockets of filling, pushing out any air bubbles. Using a pasta wheel or sharp knife, cut into squares. Place on a floured tea towel and leave to stand for 1 hour.

Bring a large pan of salted water to the boil. Add the ravioli, bring back to the boil and cook for 3–4 minutes, until tender. Drain, toss with the oil from the sun-dried tomatoes and serve.

SERVES 4

4 garlic cloves

500 g/1 lb 2 oz pumpkin, peeled, deseeded and cut into large chunks

4 sun-dried tomatoes in oil, drained, plus 2 tbsp oil from the jar

115 g/4 oz ricotta cheese

1 tbsp finely chopped fresh rosemary

1 quantity Basic Pasta Dough (see page 8)

plain flour, for dusting

1 egg, lightly beaten

salt and pepper

GARLIC MUSHROOM RAVIOLI

SERVES 4

75 g/2¾ oz butter

50 g/1¾ oz shallots, finely chopped

3 garlic cloves, crushed

50 g/1¾ oz mushrooms, wiped and finely chopped

½ celery stick, finely chopped

25 g/1 oz pecorino cheese, finely grated, plus extra to serve

½ quantity Basic Pasta Dough (see page 8)

plain flour, for dusting

1 egg, lightly beaten

salt and pepper

Heat 25 g/1 oz of the butter in a frying pan. Add the shallots, 1 crushed garlic clove, the mushrooms and celery and cook for 4–5 minutes. Remove the frying pan from the heat, stir in the pecorino cheese and season to taste with salt and pepper.

Divide the pasta dough in half and wrap 1 piece in clingfilm. Roll out the other piece on a lightly floured surface to a rectangle 2–3 mm/¹⁄₁₆–⅛ inch thick. Cover with a damp tea towel and roll out the other piece of dough to the same size. Place small mounds, about 1 teaspoon each, of the filling in rows 4 cm/ 1½ inches apart on a sheet of pasta dough. Brush the spaces between the mounds with the beaten egg. Lift the second sheet of dough on top of the first and press down firmly between the pockets of filling, pushing out any air bubbles. Using a pasta wheel or sharp knife, cut into squares. Place on a floured tea towel and leave to stand for 1 hour.

Bring a large heavy-based saucepan of water to the boil, add the ravioli and cook in batches for 2–3 minutes, or until cooked. Remove with a slotted spoon and drain thoroughly.

Meanwhile, melt the remaining butter in a frying pan. Add the remaining garlic and plenty of pepper and cook for 1–2 minutes. Transfer the ravioli to serving plates and pour over the garlic butter. Garnish with grated pecorino cheese and serve immediately.

SPINACH
& RICOTTA
RAVIOLI

Place the spinach in a heavy-based saucepan with just the water clinging to the leaves after washing, then cover and cook over a low heat for 5 minutes, until wilted. Drain well and squeeze out as much moisture as possible. Leave to cool, then chop finely. Beat the ricotta until smooth, then stir in the spinach, Parmesan and 1 of the eggs and season with nutmeg and pepper.

Divide the pasta dough in half and wrap 1 piece in clingfilm. Roll out the other piece on a lightly floured surface to a rectangle 2–3 mm/¹⁄₁₆–¹⁄₈ inch thick. Cover with a damp tea towel and roll out the other piece of dough to the same size. Place small mounds, about 1 teaspoon each, of the filling in rows 4 cm/1½ inches apart on a sheet of pasta dough. In a small bowl, lightly beat the remaining egg and use it to brush the spaces between the mounds. Lift the second sheet of dough on top of the first and press down firmly between the pockets of filling, pushing out any air bubbles. Using a pasta wheel or sharp knife, cut into squares. Place on a floured tea towel and leave to stand for 1 hour.

Bring a large heavy-based saucepan of lightly salted water to the boil, add the ravioli, in batches, return to the boil and cook for 5 minutes. Remove with a slotted spoon and drain on kitchen paper. Transfer to a warmed serving dish and serve immediately, sprinkled with Parmesan cheese.

SERVES 4

350 g/12 oz spinach leaves, coarse stalks removed

225 g/8 oz ricotta cheese

55 g/2 oz freshly grated Parmesan cheese, plus extra to serve

2 eggs

pinch of freshly grated nutmeg

1 quantity Spinach Pasta Dough (see page 8)

plain flour, for dusting

salt and pepper

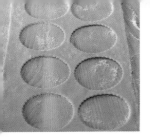

VEGETABLE RAVIOLI

To make the filling, cut the aubergines and the courgettes into 2.5-cm/1-inch chunks. Place the aubergine pieces in a colander, sprinkle with salt and leave for about 20 minutes. Rinse and drain, then pat dry on kitchen paper.

Blanch the tomatoes in boiling water for 2 minutes. Drain, peel and chop the flesh. Core and deseed the peppers and cut into 2.5-cm/1-inch dice. Chop the garlic and onion.

Heat the oil in a large pan over a low heat. Add the garlic and onion and cook for 3 minutes. Stir in the aubergines, courgettes, tomatoes, peppers, tomato purée and chopped basil. Season to taste with salt and pepper, cover and simmer for 20 minutes.

Roll out the pasta dough on a lightly floured surface to a rectangle 2–3 mm/$\frac{1}{16}$–$\frac{1}{8}$ inch thick. Using a 5-cm/2-inch plain biscuit cutter, stamp out rounds. Place small mounds, about 1 teaspoon each, of the filling on half of the rounds. Brush the edges with a little water, then cover with the remaining rounds, pressing the edges to seal. Place on a floured tea towel and leave to stand for 1 hour. Preheat the oven to 200°C/400°F/Gas Mark 6.

Bring a large pan of lightly salted water to the boil over a medium heat. Add the ravioli and cook for about 3–4 minutes. Drain and transfer to a greased ovenproof dish, dotting each layer with butter. Pour over the cream and sprinkle over the Parmesan. Bake in the preheated oven for 20 minutes. Garnish with basil and serve.

SERVES 4

2 large aubergines

3 large courgettes

6 large tomatoes

1 large green pepper

1 large red pepper

3 garlic cloves

1 large onion

125 ml/4 fl oz olive oil

4½ tsp tomato purée

½ tsp chopped fresh basil, plus extra sprigs to garnish

1 quantity Basic Pasta Dough (see page 8)

plain flour, for dusting

6 tbsp butter

150 ml/5 fl oz single cream

85 g/3 oz freshly grated Parmesan cheese

salt and pepper

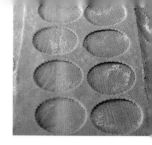

CREAMY CHICKEN RAVIOLI

SERVES 4

115 g/4 oz cooked skinless, boneless chicken breast, roughly chopped

55 g/2 oz cooked spinach

55 g/2 oz prosciutto, roughly chopped

1 shallot, roughly chopped

6 tbsp freshly grated pecorino cheese

pinch of freshly grated nutmeg

2 eggs, lightly beaten

1 quantity Basic Pasta Dough (see page 8)

plain flour, for dusting

300 ml/10 fl oz double cream

2 garlic cloves, finely chopped

115 g/4 oz chestnut mushrooms, thinly sliced

2 tbsp shredded fresh basil, plus extra sprigs to garnish

salt and pepper

Place the chicken, spinach, prosciutto and shallot in a food processor and process until chopped and blended. Transfer to a bowl, stir in 2 tablespoons of the pecorino cheese, the nutmeg and 1 of the eggs. Season to taste with salt and pepper.

Divide the pasta dough in half and wrap 1 piece in clingfilm. Roll out the other piece on a lightly floured surface to a rectangle 2–3 mm/$\frac{1}{16}$–$\frac{1}{8}$ inch thick. Cover with a damp tea towel and roll out the other piece of dough to the same size. Place small mounds, about 1 teaspoon each, of the filling in rows 4 cm/1½ inches apart on a sheet of pasta dough. Brush the spaces between the mounds with the remaining beaten egg. Lift the second sheet of dough on top of the first and press down firmly between the pockets of filling, pushing out any air bubbles. Using a pasta wheel or sharp knife, cut into squares. Place on a floured tea towel and leave to stand for 1 hour.

Bring a large saucepan of lightly salted water to the boil. Add the ravioli in batches and cook for 5 minutes. Remove with a slotted spoon, drain and transfer to a warmed dish.

Meanwhile, pour the cream into a frying pan, add the garlic and bring to the boil. Simmer for 1 minute, then add the mushrooms and 2 tablespoons of the remaining cheese. Season and simmer for 3 minutes. Stir in the basil, then pour the sauce over the ravioli. Sprinkle with the remaining cheese, garnish with basil and serve.

CHICKEN
& BACON
TORTELLINI

Melt the butter in a large heavy-based frying pan. Add the chicken, pork and pancetta and cook over a medium heat, stirring frequently, until lightly browned. Remove from the pan and leave to cool slightly, then transfer to a food processor. Add the sausage, Parmesan and 1 of the eggs and process until chopped and blended. Scrape the mixture into a large bowl and season with the mixed spice, salt and pepper.

Roll out the pasta dough on a lightly floured surface to a rectangle 2–3 mm/$\frac{1}{16}$–$\frac{1}{8}$ inch thick. Cover with a damp tea towel and roll out the other piece of dough to the same thickness. Using a 5-cm/2-inch plain biscuit cutter, stamp out rounds. Place about 1 teaspoon of the prepared filling in the centre of each round. Brush the edges of each round with a little beaten egg, then fold them in half to make half moons and press the edges to seal. Wrap a half moon around the tip of your index finger until the corners meet and press them together to seal. Repeat with the remaining pasta half moons. Place the filled tortellini on a floured tea towel and leave to stand for 1 hour.

Bring a pan of lightly salted water to the boil. Add the tortellini in batches, return to the boil and cook for 10 minutes. Remove with a slotted spoon and drain on kitchen paper, then transfer to a warmed serving dish. Sprinkle the tortellini with the extra grated Parmesan cheese and serve immediately.

SERVES 6

15 g/½ oz butter

115 g/4 oz skinless, boneless chicken breast, diced

115 g/4 oz pork fillet, diced

115 g/4 oz pancetta or rindless streaky bacon, diced

55 g/2 oz mortadella sausage, roughly chopped

115 g/4 oz freshly grated Parmesan cheese, plus extra to serve

2 eggs, lightly beaten

pinch of ground mixed spice

2 quantities Basic Pasta Dough (see page 8)

plain flour, for dusting

salt and pepper

CHICKEN TORTELLINI

Bring a saucepan of water to the boil. Add the chicken and poach for 10 minutes. Leave to cool slightly, then put in a food processor with the Parma ham, spinach and onion and process until finely chopped. Stir in 2 tablespoons of the Parmesan, the allspice and 1 of the eggs and season with salt and pepper.

Roll out the pasta dough on a lightly floured surface to a rectangle 2–3 mm/$\frac{1}{16}$–$\frac{1}{8}$ inch thick. Using a 5-cm/2-inch plain biscuit cutter, stamp out rounds. Place about 1 teaspoon of the filling in the centre of each round. Brush the edges with a little beaten egg, then fold in half to make a half moon, pressing the edges to seal. Wrap the half moon around the tip of your index finger until the corners meet and press them together to seal. Repeat with the remaining pasta half moons. Place the filled tortellini on a floured tea towel and leave to stand for 1 hour.

Bring a pan of lightly salted water to a boil. Add the tortellini in batches and cook for 10 minutes. Remove with a slotted spoon and drain on kitchen paper, then transfer to a serving dish.

To make the sauce, bring the cream and garlic to the boil in a small pan, then simmer for 3 minutes. Add the mushrooms and 2 tablespoons of the Parmesan, season to taste with salt and pepper and simmer for 2–3 minutes. Pour the sauce over the tortellini. Sprinkle over the remaining Parmesan, garnish with the parsley and serve.

SERVES 4

115 g/4 oz skinless, boneless chicken breast

55 g/2 oz Parma ham

40 g/1½ oz cooked spinach, well drained

1 tbsp finely chopped onion

6 tbsp freshly grated Parmesan cheese

pinch of ground allspice

2 eggs, beaten

2 quantities Basic Pasta Dough (see page 8)

plain flour, for dusting

300 ml/10 fl oz single cream

2 garlic cloves, crushed

115 g/4 oz button mushrooms, thinly sliced

salt and pepper

2 tbsp chopped fresh parsley, to garnish

BEEF RAVIOLI

SERVES 6

3 tbsp olive oil

70 g/2½ oz butter

350 g/12 oz stewing beef, in a
single piece

1 red onion, finely chopped

1 celery stick, finely chopped

1 carrot, finely chopped

150 ml/5 fl oz red wine

225 ml/8 fl oz beef stock

1 tbsp tomato purée

55 g/2 oz fresh breadcrumbs

4 tbsp freshly grated Parmesan
cheese

pinch of freshly grated nutmeg

pinch of ground cinnamon

2 eggs, lightly beaten

1½ quantities Basic Pasta Dough
(see page 8)

plain flour, for dusting

salt and pepper

Heat the oil and half the butter in a large saucepan. Add the beef and cook over a medium heat for 8–10 minutes. Remove the beef from the pan. Reduce the heat and add the onion, celery and carrot to the pan. Cook for 5 minutes, until softened. Return the beef to the pan, add the wine and cook until reduced by two thirds. Combine the stock and tomato purée, stir into the pan and season. Cover and simmer very gently for 3 hours, until the meat is tender and the sauce has thickened. Remove the beef from the pan and leave to cool slightly.

Mix the breadcrumbs and half the Parmesan and stir in about half the sauce (discard the remaining sauce). Finely chop the beef and stir it into the breadcrumb mixture. Season and stir in the nutmeg, cinnamon and eggs.

Roll out the pasta dough on a lightly floured surface to 2–3 mm/ ¹⁄₁₆–¹⁄₈ inch thick. Using a fluted 5-cm/2-inch biscuit cutter, stamp out rounds. Place about 1 teaspoon of the beef mixture in the centre of each round, brush the edges with water, and fold in half, pressing the edges to seal. Place on a floured tea towel and leave to stand for 30 minutes.

Bring a pan of salted water to the boil. Add the ravioli and cook for 5–8 minutes, until tender. Meanwhile, melt the remaining butter. Drain the ravioli and place in a serving dish. Pour over the melted butter, sprinkle with the remaining Parmesan and serve.

CRAB RAVIOLI

Thinly slice the spring onions, keeping the white and green parts separate. Mix the green spring onions, crabmeat, ginger and chilli sauce to taste together in a bowl. Cover and chill.

Place the tomatoes in a food processor and process to a purée. Place the garlic, white spring onions and vinegar in a saucepan and add the puréed tomatoes. Bring to the boil, then reduce the heat and simmer for 10 minutes. Remove from the heat and reserve.

Divide the pasta dough in half and wrap 1 piece in clingfilm. Roll out the other piece on a lightly floured surface to a rectangle 2–3 mm/¹⁄₁₆–¹⁄₈ inch thick. Cover with a damp tea towel and roll out the other piece of dough to the same size. Place small mounds, about 1 teaspoon each, of the filling in rows 4 cm/ 1½ inches apart on a sheet of pasta dough. Brush the spaces between the mounds with beaten egg. Lift the second sheet of dough on top of the first and press down firmly between the pockets of filling, pushing out any air bubbles. Using a pasta wheel or sharp knife, cut into squares. Place on a floured tea towel and leave to stand for 1 hour.

Bring a large saucepan of lightly salted water to the boil. Add the ravioli and cook for 5 minutes. Remove with a slotted spoon and drain on kitchen paper. Gently heat the tomato sauce and whisk in the cream. Place the ravioli on serving plates, pour over the sauce, garnish with shredded spring onion and serve.

SERVES 4

6 spring onions

350 g/12 oz crabmeat

2 tsp finely chopped fresh ginger

¹⁄₈–¹⁄₄ tsp chilli sauce or Tabasco sauce

700 g/1 lb 9 oz tomatoes, peeled, deseeded and roughly chopped

1 garlic clove, finely chopped

1 tbsp white wine vinegar

1 quantity Basic Pasta Dough (see page 8)

plain flour, for dusting

1 egg, lightly beaten

2 tbsp double cream

salt

shredded spring onion, to garnish

INDEX